❧*Maria's Story*

To Marjorie
With all my best
Wishes Maria Segal
8-3-2010 Santa Barbara

❧ Maria's Story

CHILDHOOD MEMORIES OF THE HOLOCAUST

Maria Segal

BoehmGroup

Linking Past, Present, and Future

SANTA BARBARA, CALIFORNIA, 2009

ISBN 978-0-9768008-2-8

Published by Boehm Group
www.boehmgroup.com
Post Office Box 30133
Santa Barbara, CA 93130
TEL/FAX: 805-965-9889

In memory of
my beloved parents, grandparents,
brothers, sisters, Uncle Abraham
and all other relatives
who perished in
the Holocaust

∾

This book is dedicated to
my beloved children:

Michelle, Laura and Glen
And their spouses Scott, Ken and Lauren

∾

My beloved six grandchildren:

Isabel, Alex, Anna, Zachary, Jack, and Lindsey

∾

My beloved cousins:

Marie and Mauarice Najman
my Uncle Abraham

∾

And my rescuer,

Wanda and her husband

ACKNOWLEDGMENTS

Special thanks to Rachel Altman for her typing and editing work, to Martha Hassenplug for typing assistance, to Isabel Greer for creating the cover painting for this book, and to Judy Arsht for proofreading. To Virginia Durbeck for her constructive criticism, to Eric Boehm for his consulting, to Jean Olsen, Rachel Cohen, Lynn Alonso and to all others who helped make this book possible.

❧ Contents

A section of photographs follows page 38

❧ Preface

THE MAIN REASON for writing this story is to preserve my heritage for my children and to honor my parents as well as other relatives who perished in the Holocaust.

Genocide of Jews and other nations must never happen again.

This must be a lesson to future generations. Hitler was an evil man and he inspired other Germans to carry out the "Final Solution"—the destruction of all Jews in Europe, in addition to many other non-Jews of whom Hitler disapproved: gypsies, homosexuals, the handicapped and the mentally ill.

Hitler considered the Germans a superior race. When Hitler became chancellor of Germany in 1933, his plan was to eliminate all European Jews and other individuals of whom he disapproved politically or socially.

Hitler established concentration camps in Germany and Poland. When he invaded Poland in September of 1939, he established ghettos in European cities so he could round up all the Jews and confine them in a small area. Once the Jews were confined in the ghettos, Germany had full control over their destiny: send them to the death camps—to complete what the Nazi government called "The Final Solution".

The Hitler government slaughtered 6,000,000 European Jews— most of the Jews in Europe. Perhaps he never thought that the handful of Jews who survived the ghettos and concentration camps would survive to tell the world of the atrocities and barbarity he committed against humanity.

Genocide like the Holocaust must never happen again to anyone, no matter what their race or religion—white, black, Jew or Catholic. This should be a lesson to the world: one maniac can build a large enough following to support him in genocide.

Never Again! Never Again! "Never Again" should be our motto.

Maria's Story

Chapter I

∾*My Early Childhood: 1935*

I WAS BORN into a Polish Jewish family of seven children, the second youngest of five girls and two boys. My family and I lived in Okuniew, a small farming community about ten miles from the metropolis of Warsaw.

If you remember the town of Anatevka in *Fiddler on the Roof,* you can visualize Okuniew. Similar to most small European towns, Okuniew was centered around a small plaza, a square with streets branching out in different directions like an octopus. The plaza was the commercial, political and social center and embodied the heart of the town. The main buildings consisted of an apartment house, a pharmacy, a police station, and several other small businesses. The plaza and its main streets were paved with cobblestones, while the less significant side streets were still dirt in those days. The Catholic church was prominently located on one side of the plaza. The Jewish house of prayer, the synagogue was on the other side of town. On Sundays I remember seeing Christian worshippers dressed in their finest clothes, conversing and chatting with each other about the weather and the week's events in general.

We Jews observed our Sabbath on Saturday. I remember men dressed in dark clothes, some with black hats covering their heads. They were bearded and had side-burns. The older and more Orthodox women shaved their heads and wore wigs known as *shaitels.* My mother was too modern to shave her head; she had beautiful black curly hair, as one of my sisters and I did. My other sister, Shandulka, had red

3

hair. Our synagogue was an Orthodox congregation where men and women were not permitted to sit together while praying. When I went with my family, I sat with my mother and sisters.

Jewish holidays were very colorful, especially Passover. Then my mother always made new clothes for the girls. Prior to entering the synagogue for worship, we would congregate outside the building to take note of what everyone wore, and to show off our pretty new garb acquired for the festive occasion.

My father, Lieb Polonowicz, and his family were from Okuniew. My mother Leah was from "the big city," Warsaw. She didn't fit into life in Okuniew. I think they met when my father traveled to Warsaw on business to buy leather for his shoe-making business.

My father was a very pious man. I do not recall him ever missing a Saturday morning service. My mother was not raised in an Orthodox home and was not as religious as he was. Still, she made a commitment to observe the Sabbath and the holidays in order to please my father. I recall my parents arguing at times, because my mother would not always or completely observe the rituals required for keeping a kosher house; for example, she was sometimes careless about separating meat dishes from dairy dishes. My father observed the Sabbath rigorously.

In a strictly Orthodox home, cooking is not permitted on Saturdays; therefore, all meals had to be prepared by Friday before sundown. My mother would do the cooking and baking on Friday morning and afternoon. Since we did not have our own oven at home, all the baking had to be done at the village bakery. The children would help Mother carry the cakes and pastries to the Jewish bakery, to be baked in their large ovens. I remember waiting in anticipation on Saturday afternoons, following services at the synagogue, for our main course to come out of the large communal oven. This was a dish called *chulent*, which had to be prepared on Friday and brought to the oven Friday afternoon. The *chulent* was prepared in a clay casserole dish. It consisted of brisket of beef, beans, and potatoes. Upon seasoning the food and adding some water, it was covered with a clay lid, wrapped with brown paper, tied up with string and marked with our family name. Following Saturday morning services each family would stop at the bakery on the way home to retrieve this succulent dish for the feast to come. The real fun was in trying to identify the right dish, as most of them looked alike after the brown paper had burned—the likeness compounded by melted oozing grease on top. At this point the family was anxiously awaiting the serving of the meal.

The meal was taken at a large dining room table adorned by a traditional white damask tablecloth. Of course, we must not forget the traditional Sabbath bread called *challah*. The *challah* is always served preceding the meal. My father would make a blessing, a *moitza*, over this special bread, and break off small pieces of it to be passed around to each family member seated at the table.

Saturday was a day of rest. It usually consisted of spending the afternoon around the house reading, or taking a walk. There was no television or radio then for diversion; in fact we had no electricity or indoor plumbing—not unusual for the houses then. The entire village did not have electricity or running water. There was a *mikva*, a ritual bath, at the temple that my parents might have used, but I remember bathing in a wooden tub in the kitchen once a week.

I was named Miriam in those days, and I was the second youngest girl and very close to my father. The youngest in the family was my sister Sonja. My father was a short man and very dedicated to all of us. I remember walking with him in the nearby fields on Saturday afternoons, after the synagogue. He would hold my hand; sometimes we talked and other times he would go on praying. I looked forward to our walks all week, because my father was too busy working during the week to be able to spend much time with me.

My brothers, Moishe and Yoseph, and my sisters, Nicha, Elka, and Shandulka, were considerably older than I was. Often they had friends visiting at our house, or they would all go out to someone else's home. My parents must have been very accepting socially, as I recall frequent gatherings of young people at the Polonowicz household. There was no other entertainment for young people in those days—no movie theaters, no TV to watch. We had to amuse each other.

Passover (lasting eight days) always brings back some very special memories for me. It is a truly unique holiday because of the multiple rituals involved in its preparation. Prior to its onset, all dishes and kitchen utensils had to be scrubbed and cleaned in a major sterilization process. In our daily use we had two sets of dishes, one for meat and the other for dairy products. On Passover we had to use dishes that had never been used with bread or other leavened products, so-called *chumetz*. Some of the more affluent families had a separate set of Passover dishes, which were only used during those eight days but most families had to undergo the rigorous cleansing process of the everyday dishes. In those days it took a great deal of ingenuity to accomplish this task, since we had no running water. After fetching water from the village well in buckets, it was heated in large pans on the potbelly stove and poured into a large wooden tub. This tub had multiple other uses, including laundry and bathing. A good-sized rock was heated with the water so it would retain more heat. Next, all our dishes, pots, pans and other kitchen utensils were placed in the tub with the hot water. The tub was generally placed on the lawn in the back yard. After an hour or two, the dishes were considered sterilized and ready for Passover use.

The next step was to clean the house. The floors were well scrubbed, then covered with newspapers. Everyone had to search for any remaining bread in the house. Passover began at sundown and the *chumetz* (bread products) had to be replaced by noon by *matzos*, the unleavened bread. My older sisters were teenagers and helped my mother, while I got into trouble.

The evening Passover meal, the "Seder," entailed gathering at the dinner table. Many persons were present and numerous traditional dishes were served. It was customary to share the Passover meal with a stranger who has no family to be with. Depending on the religiosity of a particular family, a Seder can last anywhere from one to several hours. My father was Orthodox in his upbringing, hence generally took his time in conducting the Seder. Wine was served in abundance. My father made his own red wine. Prior to Passover I would often see jars of cherries fermenting on window sills.

The true joy of the Seder was to bring the many family members together: aunts, uncles, cousins and grandparents. All participants partake in the ritual prayers prior to the distribution of the many special foods. Many times during the course of the Seder our mouths salivated in anticipation of the moment when the meal was to be served. Some of the traditional Seder foods include hard-boiled eggs, greens, bitter herbs, wine, *matzos*, and of course, chicken soup with dumplings, called *kneidle* or matzo balls. Brisket was a traditional main dish, or chicken served with roasted potatoes and sweet carrots.

The many rituals and special foods of the Jewish religion play a major role in this observance. Almost every holiday has its characteristic foods. For instance on Hanukah, the Festival of Lights, the traditional dish is potato pancakes, or *latkes*. There are many other religious holidays with numerous traditions. On Purim we had plates of *hamantashen* (turnovers filled with fruit) with poppy seeds.

As a young child I was very happy to be part of a large family. Until my younger sister Sonja came along, my older siblings paid a lot of attention to me. Naturally, I did not have much responsibility as far as household chores; the older sisters and brothers did everything for me and I always had my younger sister to play with. I enjoyed being around my older siblings and their friends. I am sure at times I must have been an annoying little pest.

I started school at a young age. I do not believe there were specific guidelines as to age requirements. The first language I grew up with was Yiddish. When I started school I had to speak Polish. Apparently I was a fast learner. I remember my first parent-teacher conference. I had a male teacher and he told my mother that I had a *"yiddishe kopf,"* a Jewish head. My recollections of the rest of school are a little fuzzy. The town of Okuniew also had a *cheder*, a Jewish parochial school. My older siblings attended cheder. I was still too young.

Okuniew was a small village and we all knew each other, especially the Jewish people, as everybody went to the same synagogue. My father was a shoemaker. My brothers worked with my father. My grandfather and my two uncles had their own shop. My father also had a couple of other young men working in his shop. It was a trade passed down from generation to generation. His shop was in the front of the house facing the plaza. My family lived in the back of the shop. I liked to hang around the shop and meet some of my father's customers.

I recall meeting two elegant well-to-do ladies who had their shoes repaired by my father. They had a carriage and horses and servants. They lived in a very large home, a beautifully landscaped estate with huge gates. On one occasion the two ladies came to the shop and they befriended me. They invited me to visit their chateau and I was absolutely delighted. I will never forget when I went for the visit and took the repaired shoes to them. I had never seen a big beautiful house like that before. I was totally mesmerized, and most of all I fell in love with the spiral staircase. I walked up and down the staircase with sheer delight. I was invited to have tea and sweets with them on the luxurious veranda. My siblings were very jealous that I was invited to see the chateau and they wanted a detailed account of everything I did and saw.

From time to time my father went to Warsaw on business to buy leather for the shoes and boots that his clients ordered. On several occasions he took me with him on the train and I enjoyed spending that special time with him. It was very novel to me to be in a large city with electricity and running water.

My mother, like my father, was very devoted to the family. I enjoyed spending time with her. She was very loving—she would hug and kiss Sonja and me, and made us feel special. She spent a great deal of time preparing our meals and taking care of our large family. I loved watching her in the kitchen and going grocery shopping with her. We had to go to a butcher to buy kosher meat. At times, on Friday mornings we went to buy chickens and I witnessed the chicken being slaughtered. I did not like that part at all. According to Jewish tradition, for meat to be kosher it has to be slaughtered by a *shoichet*, a special Jewish butcher, in accordance with Jewish rituals and laws.

We lived successively in three houses in Okuniew. The first was a small cottage with cherry trees and grass in the backyard. We had "our own" pump for water and "our own" out-house. I remember it as being on the outskirts of town.

Our second house was an apartment where "the accident" occurred. There my sister Shandulka, "the red-head," fell into a tub of scalding water and burned the side of her leg. We then moved to a larger house facing the plaza where my father had a shop in front and we lived in the back. It was all on one floor. We got water from the village pump. The back of the house had a kitchen with two beds that Sonja and I slept in, a bedroom for the boys, and a separate bedroom for my parents. I vaguely remember one other room—maybe it was for the older girls.

In the backyard we had trees. I loved climbing trees. I was obnoxious at times and wanted to eat my food in the tree, and when my mom asked me to come down, I refused. I made my mom angry at times. I guess I had no fear and was somewhat of a tomboy. I would climb to the "tippy-top" of the cherry tree and shake the very thin branches; I loved to eat the cherries. My mother was terrified and yelled at me to come down. To this day I like to buy cherries when they are available; today my children buy me cherries because they know how much I enjoy them.

I seemed to have a great deal of energy as a child and felt very alive. I was a carefree bird enjoying the outdoors and my freedom to run around.

Chapter II

ᴏᴡ *The Onset of World War II*

I WAS A CHILD of five when Germany invaded Poland in 1939. I recall a lot of commotion at home and in the neighborhood. There was a sense of restlessness among the people—much talk, speculation, and chit-chat regarding what would happen when the Germans took over Poland. Everyone was worried about the scarcity of food when the war broke out. Since we lived in a farming community, we could generally count on an ample supply of potatoes, bread, milk and meat—the basics, but no luxuries.

Because my father was a shoemaker, he was able to repair shoes in exchange for food. I remember eating a lot of potatoes and meat after the war broke out.

Shortly after the invasion, the Germans began to put restrictions on Jews. First, I was not allowed to attend public schools. Second, in order to further single us out, we had to wear white armbands printed with a large yellow Star of David. Before I went out of the house I had to put the armband on.

The Germans did not permit the Jewish children to study at all. Consequently we had to meet secretly in *cheders*, parochial schools. I was young at the time; however, I remember meeting at the teacher's house, the Rebbe of Okuniew. This dedicated teacher risked his life when he took it upon himself to perpetuate Judaism through his teachings and to provide the village children with continuing education.

As soon as the Germans entered Okuniew, they took away my

father's younger brother, our uncle Moishe. This frightened my grand-father so much that he died from a heart attack. Grandfather was a *shames* who took care of the synagogue; he was buried in the local Jew-ish cemetery next to the Catholic church and cemetery. I did not go to the funeral, but was very upset as I loved my grandpa dearly. Grandpa and Grandma lived a few doors away from us and I used to go to their house often. My uncle Moishe and his family and children also lived nearby. All of them were taken to the Warsaw Ghetto. I never saw them again. I do not know if they died in the ghetto or on the way to it.

It seemed that everything in those days was scary and secretive. Wherever we went there were German soldiers parading around in their green uniforms and helmets, with carbines hanging over their shoulders. They always had fierce dogs. They never smiled much, al-ways looking angry and unapproachable. This tense atmosphere hung over the community for weeks, maybe even months.

One evening there was a lot of commotion in town. The adults were rushing around, talking to neighbors, blank looks on their trou-bled faces. Of course we children became agitated and wanted to ask questions, but we were afraid to because of the tension in the air. Fi-nally, late that evening, my parents gathered all the children around the pot-bellied stove and broke the news to us about the unrest. Rumor had it that the Germans were planning to round up all the Jews in town and deport them to the Warsaw Ghetto.

"It's possible that it may happen very soon," I remember hear-ing someone say, "Maybe even as soon as tomorrow morning." People were very frightened as to what fate would hold for them. Apparently a number of Jews, who had some money, planned to leave that night for Russia or some other country that was not under German occu-pation.

My parents were very upset and worried as they tried to prepare us as well as they could for the possibility of being separated. My older brothers and sisters were put in charge of looking after my younger sister and me. My mother and older sisters sewed little satchels for the few belongings we could take. They made nametags with strings to hang around our necks. In each satchel we placed a few of our treasures and precious belongings, along with bits and pieces of food that we had in the house.

Our parents instructed us to stay together if possible, and told us that if we were taken to the Warsaw Ghetto, we should meet at our uncle's house. My mother had two brothers living in Warsaw and was sure we could live with them. We all had a very restless night, interrupted in the early hours of the morning by rasping German voices shouting through loudspeakers for all Jews to leave their homes and congregate at the town plaza. What a terrible sight, young and old with their worldly possessions on their backs, clinging to each other and trying to obey the German commands.

From then on, it got worse by the minute. The solders had their snarling German shepherd dogs helping them group the frightened townspeople. They had small wooden wagons hitched to horses in which to transport the women and children. The first bad and sad thing that happened to me was that I was separated from my mother and father. My father had to go to the side with the men, as did my oldest brother Moshe. My mother was made to go on a different wagon.

I was in the wagon with one of my older sisters, Shandulka. We did not know where the rest of the family was. I was frightened and my sister was extremely upset. I tried to console her as best I could. In the meantime, the Germans separated the men from the women and children, yelling at us, and we heard shots in the distance as we rode away on the carts.

It took a whole day to get to Warsaw. When we finally reached the Warsaw Ghetto, the Germans immediately had us take off our clothes. They herded us into communal showers—men, women and children. I was very scared; I did not understand what was happening. Then a fortunate thing happened: my whole family found each other in the showers. I was thrilled to be with my mother, father, sisters and brothers.

In the Ghetto we were more fortunate than other families, as we went straight to Nowolipki Street where my uncle Itzak and his family lived in a small apartment with two grown children. My uncle gave us one small room and all nine of us stayed there. There was only one bed.

My parents slept in the bed and all of us took the floor. Though it was crowded, we had a roof over our heads. Most of the people who did not have relatives had to find a place to stay or be on the streets.

The apartment was in a wonderful house with electricity, an elevator and flush toilets. I loved the elevator, and went up and down as often as I wanted. The toilet had a tank on top with a chain; I loved pulling the chain.

Outside the apartment, the Ghetto was not a pretty sight, with skeleton-like people wandering the streets and keeling over from hunger or sickness. No provisions were made to bury them. Corpses were covered with paper and carted away on small wagons. It was a shock for me to see this. I was devastated.

Chapter III

◈ *In the Warsaw Ghetto: 1940*

ABOUT 500,000 JEWS were confined in the Warsaw Ghetto, which consisted of several city streets surrounded by tall brick walls, with barbed wire and glass on top to prevent any escape. The Jews from Warsaw and the surrounding areas were brought into the Ghetto, dumped and left to fend for themselves.

Jews were not permitted to leave the Ghetto. In some places one could find openings, heavily guarded by the Gestapo on the Polish side and by the Jewish militia inside the Ghetto walls. Gentiles were permitted to enter the Ghetto for business purposes. Many Gentiles took advantage of the situation by exchanging food for furs and jewels if cash was unavailable. Very often people would give anything they had for a piece of bread. The only goal at this point was survival, and it was most certainly a survival of the fittest.

My family had to find ways of sustaining ourselves. Our relatives were struggling to support their own household and were in no position to feed nine additional mouths. Food was scarce and extremely dear, and employment was difficult to find. Almost every member of my family had to seek employment to be able to buy food. My father and two older brothers were fortunate enough to find a shoemaker who was willing to give them jobs. I can't recall what they earned, I just heard the family talk about how little money they were able to bring home. My three older sisters found some kind of work in the clothing business. Even I, as a child of six, worked by holding yarn for a lady—my two hands stretched out in front of me so she could make it into a ball.

The only members of my family who did not hold jobs were my mother and my younger sister Sonja. Sonja was too young to work, as she was only three or four years old. My mother was not well, so she stayed home to take care of Sonja, the house, and the marketing.

On occasion I would go to the market with my mother and sister. It was an outdoor market and my mother would complain about how expensive even potatoes were. At times many staples were unavailable, depending what the farmers brought in that day from the nearby Gentile villages. Mother tried her best to obtain food to sustain the family with the limited resources we had. Most of the time mother fed us soup—usually very watery. Bread was a true luxury, and we all lined up in the kitchen to get a piece. My mother rationed it very carefully, as there was usually not enough to go around more than once. There were many times, however, when we did not have enough for even a ration of one piece of bread per person. Since carrots were relatively inexpensive by comparison, my mother bought more carrots than anything else and we would crunch away on them like rabbits. To this day, I hate carrots with a passion. They bring back memories of the Warsaw Ghetto and an endlessly empty stomach.

Even though our whole family of nine occupied one small room, we were still more fortunate than others who entered the Ghetto without any relatives already living there. At least we had a roof over our heads and a little food to sustain ourselves. Many people did not have enough food to feed themselves and had no place to live. Many roamed the streets searching the garbage cans for a few morsels of food to be consumed. Some of the people walking the streets were so emaciated that they resembled human skeletons, clad in rags. I was extremely saddened to see these unfortunate human beings hardly able to walk and collapsing on the street when they were too weak to move their muscles any longer. Even though I was a child, it made me pause to think about the value of life and of the vulnerability and helplessness of human beings.

So many of these innocent poor souls not only starved to death, but were unable to get a decent burial when they finally died. Once the bodies collapsed, they were covered with newspapers lying on the street, and after a time, their skeletons were loaded onto wheelbarrows and carted off, most likely to the nearest dump. No one really cared or worried about what happened to anyone else: We were all too concerned with our own survival.

Because of the bodies lying on the streets, at times the stench was very pungent and disease common. Typhoid reached epidemic proportions. Medical help was almost nonexistent, and besides, no one could afford to pay a doctor. We hoped and prayed not to get sick.

Housing was expensive and crowded conditions prevailed. Furthermore, the Ghetto was shrinking; the Germans decided to make it smaller and subsequently eliminated several streets. Then they began to deport Jews from the Ghetto. They did not tell people where they were taking them. The typical explanation was that they were taking them to labor camps. Each day the Germans rounded up hundreds of men, women and children, loaded them into trains and took them to concentration camps in Poland: Auschwitz, Treblinka, Majdanek and others.

Most of the Germans stayed out of the Ghetto and selected groups of Jewish men to perform most of the administrative tasks and carry out German orders. This "elite group" of Jews made up the Jewish militia and the governing board. They also served as informers when the time came to round up Jews and send them to the concentration camps. In return, these Jews received special privileges that the ordinary person did not have.

When no one returned from these deportations, the Jews began to sense that something was wrong: the Jews taken on the trains were not coming back. It was then that the handful of remaining Jews in the Ghetto formed a group of resistance fighters. Even though they did not have access to weapons, they used all possible means to arm themselves and create ammunitions in whatever shape and form they could. They certainly had to be very creative. The Molotov cocktail was very popular, as were homemade grenades and bombs. This handful of Jews, under the able leadership of Mordecai Anielewicz, fought back in April 1943. The struggle lasted 28 days—until they were defeated.

Fortunately or unfortunately—I am not sure which was better—I did not remain in the Ghetto to the bitter end of the fighting and liquidation. A Gentile woman from Okuniew named Stasia entered the Ghetto about once a week. Stasia was a businesswoman who took advantage of the fact that the Jews in the Ghetto were desperate for food, and she would bring food in exchange for money or valuables.

Stasia came to the Ghetto and asked my mother if I could go back with her to Okuniew to look after her cow. It was decided that I would leave the ghetto with Stasia; in this way I could help my family. Some of my father's customers owed him money for shoe repairs and shoes he had made for them when we lived in Okuniew prior to deportation. I went out to the surrounding villages and collected what he was owed and was able to amass some food and money to bring to my family. I did this twice and my family was overjoyed when I returned to the Ghetto with bread, potatoes, and even some chickens. We had a true feast.

The third time I went to Warsaw with Stasia, when we tried to get back into the Ghetto, it was impossible. Security at the walls had become extremely tight and the guards would not let us in. We tried multiple crossings in the event that some other guards would be more lenient, but we had no luck with any of them, and turned back toward Okuniew.

That was the last time I saw my family. I felt very sad and perhaps guilty that no one from my family escaped the Ghetto—except me, alone.

I will never forget my mother's expression the day I left with Stasia for the first time. My mother was standing by the kitchen window with my little sister looking on. After a few minutes' silence she said to me, "Go. You are the only one in the family that has a chance to survive, because all of us will be killed sooner or later." That really bothered me because my true intention was not to be the only one to survive. My hope was to go back and forth between the Ghetto and Okuniew and help our family to obtain food. After I lost contact with my family I could not stop thinking about my mother's last words to me.

I have been riddled with guilt for surviving. I miss my family terribly, even though they have been lost for over 60 years. I can't forget them; they are constant reminders. As I reflect on those memories, I can almost see my mother standing by the kitchen window, although I can hardly recall what she looked like. Too many years have passed for me to have a clear view of her sweet, gentle and loving face.

The part of my life that I miss the most is not having my family. There is nothing in this world that can replace the loss of parents. It is still very hard for me to accept the fact that they disappeared from my life, vanished forever and I do not even know how they died or where to look for their remains.

CHAPTER IV

◦∿*Return to Okuniew: 1941*

WHEN I ARRIVED in Okuniew, I went to live with Stasia and her husband Janek. The first few days in Okuniew were sheer torture for me. The thought of being cut off from my parents, sisters and brothers and the notion that I might never see them again was devastating. As the days went on, I was more and more preoccupied, thinking about my family and worrying what might become of them.

I had daily recurring dreams about various members of my family, especially my mother. One afternoon, as I sat outdoors reflecting about my experiences, I got a little drowsy and fell asleep. When I awoke, I was very frightened. In my dream I saw my mother, and when I tried to talk to her, she did not respond; she looked like a piece of marble and I could not communicate to her how much I missed her and how much I needed her to be part of my life. The nightmares continued. At times I would wake up in the middle of the night crying. It was very difficult for me to accept my separation from my family. I refused to accept the fact that my family might perish any time and that I might never be able to see them again.

Shortly after I left the Warsaw Ghetto, I was outdoors watching the sunset. In the distance I could see red flames jutting out from burning houses in the Ghetto. I felt helpless and sad. My family might be in trouble and I could not help them. From Okuniew, I watched the Ghetto burn.

Stasia and Janek owned a one-bedroom house on a small piece of property. They had no children; they owned a skinny cow named

Betsy. The reason that Stasia took me out of the Ghetto is because she needed someone to take care of Betsy when she traveled back and forth to the Warsaw Ghetto. My responsibility was to take the black and white cow into the pasture every morning and bring her home in the evening, in time to be milked. Each morning I got up at dawn, packed a sack of lunch, put it in a small bundle over my shoulder, and Betsy and I left for the green pasture. There I joined other boys and girls from Okuniew looking after their cows. In a sense it was fun for a while: no school and very few responsibilities.

Once we arrived at the pasture, we would find a hill to sit on so we could better see the cows when they spread out to graze. Whenever the cows moved, we moved, changing locations so as not to lose sight of them.

One afternoon, about one hour before dark, as we were ready to return home, Betsy was nowhere to be found. I looked, I called her name, but she was not to be seen. After a while, the other kids tried to help me, without much success. I was scared to return home without Betsy. I just ran out of ideas where to look. It started to get dark and it was time to return home.

When I arrived home, I tried to explain to Stasia and Janek what happened. Before I had a chance to explain, they started to yell at me. After they stopped yelling, they offered to go with me into the fields to look for Betsy. All three of us looked, called Betsy dozens of times and after an hour or two, the beast appeared out of nowhere. Oh boy! Was I ever happy to see that stupid cow. From that day on, I did not let Betsy out of my sight for a second. I watched her very carefully and luckily never lost her again.

Stasia and Janek were heavy drinkers; they loved their schnapps, especially before bedtime. In fact they made their own vodka at home from potatoes, which were in abundance in Poland. I guess that making vodka was illegal, so they rigged up an apparatus that ran all night. When Stasia and Janek had too much to drink, they often argued. At times they screamed at each other so loudly that I would get scared and run across the road to Stasia's parents' house. The Polanskys, like most of the people in Okuniew, were farmers. They had a few acres of land, a farmhouse and several heads of cattle. The Polanskys were aware that their daughter and son-in-law had drinking problems. In fact they had never liked Janek; they often said that he was a lazy, good-for-nothing man.

One day when I came to their house frightened, they asked me to stay with them and not to go back to Stasia's house. I was very happy to get away from that chaotic household. Now my responsibilities slightly increased. The Polanskys had five cows, so I had to look after six cows altogether, including old Betsy. By now, I was more experienced as a pasture girl and had learned from my mistakes to keep my eyes on the cows at all times.

As time went on, I became more used to the family; however, I never ceased to think about my parents, my sisters and brothers.

One evening, after dark, there was a knock on the door. What a wonderful welcome surprise—a familiar face from the past: Toba and her boyfriend.

Toba was a young woman around twenty; she and her parents owned a grocery store in Okuniew before 1939. We all shopped there. Like all the other Jews from this village, Toba and her family were deported to the Warsaw Ghetto at the same time as my family. When the liquidation of the Warsaw Ghetto began in April 1943, Toba and her boyfriend managed to escape Warsaw before being taken to a concentration camp. Both made their way back to Okuniew to seek refuge with the Millers, a family she knew before deportation. The Millers had an old mill that was still currently in operation.

Toba had some news for me. She told me that before she left the Ghetto, she saw her family and my family being taken from the apartment by the Germans, most likely to concentration camps in Majdanek or elsewhere. That was the current rumor as to where the Jews were being deported. Toba had felt that this was her only chance of survival—to escape before the Gestapo came for them.

Toba stayed for a short period of time. We embraced and she left cautiously, in fear of being recognized by someone in the village. She and her boyfriend returned to the Millers. Before Toba left, she gave me a snapshot of my sisters and brothers which I still treasure. I have few photographs of my family.

Two days later I was told that the Germans picked up Toba and her boyfriend from the Millers, took them to the local cemetery and shot them. Unfortunately, someone squealed on them and they had to die so young just for being Jewish. Rumors had it that another woman and a young boy were also killed at the cemetery. From then on, I began to fear for my own safety. I wondered if I would be the next victim. Although most of the Poles in the village knew my whereabouts and did nothing to harm me, I was still very scared.

A few days after the death of Toba and her boyfriend, as I sat in the kitchen with the Polanskys, there was a knock at the front door. Mrs. Polansky went to the door to ask who it was. When the voice replied, "Police and Gestapo," Mr. Polansky immediately pushed me out the back window into a cornfield and told them that I no longer lived there. When the police left, the Polanskys came out to the cornfield to bring me food and a blanket. I was afraid to spend the night there. Together we decided that it was no longer safe for me to remain in their home. Apparently, the Germans had decided to round up all the remaining Jews in town, and I was on their list. The cornfield became my living quarters for several days.

I walked to the nearby woods, remaining in hiding at all times. Mr. Polansky was very kind. He always found me and brought me food to eat. At night he came again to check on me. I could deal with the days much better, wandering around here and there in the fields or woods. When night fell, I got frightened of the dark and any slight noises echoing scared me. Once again, I experienced loneliness when thinking about my family. I continuously had bad dreams of running and being chased.

A week went by and the police did not return to the Polanskys' house for me. We decided that I could stay in the fields during the day and sleep in the attic at night. I did not like the attic at all; it was dark and spooky. I was frightened at the noises and creaks, nevertheless, I had to remain in hiding if I valued my life. More news came of a teenage boy executed when he was found out. Now, although a young child, I had to start planning where to go for safety.

Two weeks went by since the Gestapo and Polish police came to look for me. The Germans killed the other Jews in town; why would they spare me? While living in Okuniew since my time in the Ghetto,

I had made the acquaintance of a young woman and her family. Wanda was in her twenties with very pretty dark long hair and a beautiful face. Her father was a Polish policeman in town and I was certain that he was aware of my existence a long time before they came to get me.

Wanda and I would sit and talk together for hours. I also mended her stockings and she paid me a few cents from time to time. Shortly after our acquaintance, Wanda got married to Jurek, who lived in Warsaw.

After the wedding, Wanda moved to Warsaw. Before she moved, she asked me to come to live with her and her husband in Warsaw.

When my safety in the Polansky home was in jeopardy, Wanda sent word through her mother, telling me to come to Warsaw to live with her.

I had to plan my escape very carefully so as not to let the Poles recognize me. I said good-bye to my family in Okuniew and thanked them for taking care of me. After all, they risked their own life to protect me. If the Germans found out that they were harboring a Jewish child they could have killed them all.

CHAPTER V

～ *The Escape: 1944*

EARLY ONE MORNING, I packed a few of my belongings to take
with me. When it was still dark outside and everyone in the
house was asleep, I started walking towards the train station, which
was about three miles from the Polansky home. No one knew about
my plan except Wanda and her mother.

Wanda sent a note to her mother with the train schedule and the
time and place that she would meet me. I was tired of hiding and decided to take advantage of the opportunity to move to a large city where
no one knew me, to be able to better conceal my Jewish identity.

As I walked toward the station, I began to recognize some of the
people from the Okuniew village taking their wares to Warsaw for
business. The people on the train carried large milk cans, eggs, chickens and produce. I wore a kerchief on my head and tried to avoid looking at any one that I knew.

It was a short train ride, around thirty minutes. My concept of time
was a little fuzzy in those days. When I arrived in Warsaw, Wanda was
waiting for me at the station. We went directly to her grocery store in
the center of town. I was happy to see Wanda; she was warm and interested in my welfare, and we had a close relationship with each other.
The grocery store was very small and the first few days I just watched
Wanda. She was very pleasant and had a nice way with customers.

At the end of the day, we put some of the perishables away and
locked up the store. Subsequently we walked home. Now that I was
in the big city, I had a sense of safety. No one knew that I was Jew-

ish, and my "Aryan" features helped me conceal my Jewish identity. When we arrived at the apartment, dinner was waiting for us on the table. Wanda's maid, Riva, set the table and all the food was ready to be served within minutes of our arrival. Jurek walked in shortly after us, embraced Wanda and greeted me in a pleasant manner. Jurek was a tall, dark, handsome man, several years Wanda's senior, and a school-teacher at a high school in the same neighborhood where they lived. We all enjoyed Riva's dinner of roast chicken, potatoes and pudding for dessert.

After dinner, Riva showed me to my room. What a treat to sleep in a clean bed in a normal room! I slept quite well considering that it was my first day in a strange household and unfamiliar family.

Wanda's apartment was very spacious. I recall the high ceilings, shiny parquet floors, and carvings on the furniture in the dining room. Wanda's apartment was so much more luxurious than anything that I had been accustomed to in the past. In Okuniew we had to use out-door toilets; there was no electricity or running water. Here, we had all the modern conveniences, even an elevator, and flush toilets.

The next morning I got up at the same time as Wanda did. Both of us sat down at the breakfast table elegantly prepared by Riva. After breakfast, we walked over to the store again. Wanda began to teach me how to put things away and even sell some small uncomplicated items. This process of going to the store and coming home in the evening went on for several weeks. I was happy as long as Wanda was with me. No one suspected that I was Jewish and when people asked, Wanda told them that I was her daughter. Wanda was really kind to me; in time I did consider her like a mother. The days went by quickly, and my thoughts of my family diminished slightly however, I did not forget them.

The tension between the Germans and the Poles in Warsaw mounted. Bombings and air raids increased every day. One morning, as Wanda and I got ready to leave for the store, the sirens began to screech and instead of going to the store, we went down to the base-ment air shelter. On the way down, shrapnel was falling in all direc-tions. Nonetheless, we made it to the shelter safely. However, our next door neighbor, a young girl, was hit with shrapnel before she reached the shelter. She lay on the floor in a lot of pain. Fortunately for her, we had a doctor with us who worked on her immediately to remove the shrapnel from her arm. Afterwards all of us huddled close together in the dark, damp cellar, listening to the thunderous noises of dropping bombs and frantic sirens of fire engines. All of us sat patiently in the dark, hoping that the bombings would quiet down so we could return to our apartment as we always did after an air raid.

Unfortunately this time it was different. After several hours of hiding we were suddenly interrupted by two uniformed German soldiers motioning to us with their fingers: "Come, come."

There was no question in our minds of disobeying their orders and we all followed them upstairs. When we got upstairs, the Germans loaded us on their trucks and whisked us away to a large open field. At the field, they took all the men, old and young, while all women and children remained. There were rumors of the men being shot. Indeed, as we waited we heard gunshots in the near distance—echoing the unknown sad news.

The women and children tried to maintain their composure, but it was difficult. There was a lot of crying when the soldiers lined us up, their rifles pointed in our direction, the direction of the women and children.

One of the older German soldiers tried to console the frightened women and children awaiting their unknown fate. He told us that he, too, had a wife and children at home and did not enjoy his assignment. He was merely carrying out orders.

The suspense of the unknown was painful, and each minute seemed more like an hour. The guns continued to point in our direction. At the precise moment when the pointed machine guns were getting ready to fire, a miracle occurred. A tall uniformed German officer on a white horse came out of nowhere and charged in front of the firing squad. This god-like human being raised his right hand, hollering, "Halt!"

Slowly the firing squad dropped their weapons and retreated gradually, one by one. An enormous sigh of relief emanated from the frightened group of women and children.

Following this miraculous appearance of the German officer, our group was escorted to a nearby church for the night. Although the church was cold and we had to spend the night on the hard benches, hungry, we were grateful to have another chance to be alive. The question now was: what next?

The following day, early in the morning, our group was escorted by the German soldiers to Płaszów, a temporary camp, to process us for transport to a concentration camp. First, we had to submit to a medical examination conducted by a team of Polish doctors.

The doctors took it upon themselves to paint us with yellow chalk and tell the Germans that we had jaundice. Since the Germans were terrified of contagious diseases, they took the doctors' advice to let us go.

At the time of departure from Płaszów, I was on one side and Wanda was on the other side of the lines. I ran across to Wanda to make sure that we were not separated.

Now that we were out of Warsaw and spared from going to a concentration camp, we had to decide what to do next and where to go. Of course, without a home or money, that was not an easy task. In addition, as residents of Warsaw, we were still hunted down by the Germans. Wanda came up with a good idea. She remembered that her husband had paid for a summer vacation on a farm in the country. "Let's find the farm," she said, "and see if they would be willing to let us stay there while we look for Jurek." Jurek was in the Polish resistance, and we had no idea whether he was dead or alive. Wanda's younger brother was also in the resistance, and she had had word prior to our leaving Warsaw that he died in action, fighting in the Warsaw insurrection.

Wanda, her mother-in-law and I arrived at the farm in the evening around supper time. All three of us were exhausted, hungry and tired—physically and mentally. Initially, the farmer was reluctant to take care of us. After resisting for a long time, he softened a little, realizing how destitute we were, and agreed to let us stay for a while.

Life on the farm was not bad; we had plenty of potatoes and milk, some meat and bread. We all helped out with the daily chores on the farm in exchange for food and shelter.

The days went by quickly. Wanda did not want me to get too far behind in my schooling so she taught me math and reading almost daily. At this time I had been out of school for several years and had no immediate plans to attend school, as our future was very uncertain.

One evening, as Wanda was reading the newspaper, she came across a list of wounded soldiers, Polish and German. To her great surprise she saw her husband's name, Jurek. He was convalescing in a hospital in Krakow, recovering from injuries sustained during the fighting between the Poles and the Germans. Immediately we made plans to go to Krakow the following day to see Jurek. Their reunion was very exciting; they hugged and kissed each other a great deal.

As soon as Jurek started getting better, Wanda arranged for us to get a small apartment in Krakow.

We had no means of support, but as Wanda was an entrepreneur, she started a small business selling bread on the black market. Of course, I was always by her side, helping out whenever I could.

CHAPTER VI

∿ *The Russian Liberation: 1945*

THE TIME WENT BY fairly quickly, settling into our newly acquired apartment while we waited anxiously for Jurek's recovery.

The two-bedroom apartment was located on a narrow cobblestone street in an older section of Krakow, rather quaint and very convenient to the center of town. Since none of us—Wanda, Jurek's mother, or I—had many possessions, we had to start almost from scratch. During and after the war, most everything was dear and difficult to obtain. A lot of food was rationed and we often had to stand in long lines to buy our basic commodities. Our financial situation was bleak; Jurek's military pension was small. As soon as Jurek was ready to leave the hospital, he joined us in the apartment and got a part-time job teaching.

Wanda did not have the financial means to open another grocery store; nonetheless by selling bread on the black market she was able to supplement our income. I always went to the market with her to help. She also had a connection in the nearby city of Chenstochowa to bring in wool and textiles. I remember traveling there by train to buy wool and hiding it under my coat so as not to be caught by the Germans. Because I was still a small child of about ten, the Germans usually did not bother me and I was able to carry the wool and fabric under my clothes. My first train ride alone to a strange city was frightening; however, after a while, I got used to traveling alone. Wanda usually put me on the train, and the people in Chenstochowa picked me up. We somehow made ends meet. Krakow was not a permanent residence for us; we were trying to figure out where to go when life became a little more stable.

The war was still on and tension mounted between the Germans and the Russians. We listened daily to the radio for the news from the fronts. We heard bits and pieces that the Germans were capitulating, and heard that German troops were beginning to retreat from the fronts.

One evening, after we finished supper, we heard a bulletin that the war was over. The fighting had ended and the Russian troops were marching towards Krakow. We all jumped up in the air hugging and kissing each other with joy. The emotions of the thought of freedom ran high.

The following morning the Russian troops marched into Krakow. We put on our coats and walked over to the town square in the center of town. People were yelling, screaming happily as we watched the Russian troops approach the Polish Citadel. This was one of the happiest days of my life since I was separated from my parents, my sisters and brothers.

The end of war in 1945 gave me a new hope—a hope that perhaps I could find some of my family. When the excitement of greeting the Russian soldiers was over, I began to write letters to the International Red Cross in Geneva, Switzerland. People were scattered everywhere; so many people were looking for lost relatives. Special areas were set up to locate each other. I seized the opportunity to try to find my family, if any of them were still alive. Wanda also tried to find her parents, and Jurek was looking for his sister and her young son.

Jurek's sister Brenda had a bar-restaurant in the city of Bydgoszcz, a Polish city on the Baltic Sea, so we decided to venture there. The Russians had also liberated Bydgoszcz. Brenda had an apartment adjoining the restaurant and we were fortunate that she let us stay with her until we could get on our feet again.

We all helped Brenda in the restaurant. Jurek became the bartender and I helped Wanda serve. The restaurant was always busy, in particular with Russian soldiers coming in for meals. The Russians loved to party and drink vodka, and they sang and danced cheerfully.

One day a Russian officer took a liking to me at Brenda's restaurant. When he found out that I lost my whole family in the Warsaw Ghetto, he asked me to go to Moscow with him. He wanted to adopt me and take care of me in Russia. I was pleased that he liked me enough to want me to go with him; however, I had an obligation to Wanda and Jurek. They had saved my life and stuck by me during the war. Besides, I never gave up hope that some day I would find my own family.

After several months, I got a reply from the Swiss Red Cross. They had located a cousin of mine who went to Russia before the war broke out in 1939, and he was now back in Poland. I immediately wrote a letter to my cousin, my mother's nephew, thinking that he might have news of my other family members.

The reply in the letter was disappointing. It stated that my cousin had moved on and he did not leave a forwarding address. This was a big letdown to my hopes that some relatives were still alive.

In the meantime, Wanda and Jurek found a three-bedroom apartment in Bydgoszcz. We settled down little by little, and this became home for all of us. Wanda enrolled me in school; she put me in a fifth grade class although I had not attended school for all the war years, except for the lessons Wanda had taught me while we were on the farm.

The first day at school was absolutely miserable. I did not know anything. The kids laughed at me every time the teacher asked me a question and I did not know the answer. I tried not to get discouraged and instead worked very hard with the assistance of Jurek and Wanda at home. Halfway through the school year I did very well and the teacher promoted me to the sixth grade that same year. The other students no longer laughed at me; in fact, they elected me President of the Red Cross organization of my sixth grade class.

From then on, I enjoyed school and the praise that I received for my hard work. I now had several friends at school, especially a close friend by the name of Basia. Basia and I became real pals; we spent a lot of time together. We had a lot in common. She had also lost her parents and was living with her aunt. Basia did not always like her aunt and I still missed my parents as well as my sisters and brothers.

Basia and I laughed together and cried on each others' shoulders when we were sad. It was very therapeutic for Basia and me to talk. There was no secret in the world between us. Basia and I were in the same grade and she too was a good student. Whenever I became sad about my family, I got together with Basia, and we talked and cried together and felt much better afterwards.

The following year I was promoted to the seventh grade. We had a male teacher, very handsome, with dark curly black hair. All the girls had a crush on him. I continued to do well in school and as a reward for my good work; my teacher selected me to represent the school in Denmark on a two-month vacation before the completion of the school year. It was a real honor to be picked and Wanda and Jurek were proud that I was selected, and some of the other students were very jealous of me.

Wanda helped me prepare for the journey to Denmark, and her mother made some clothes for me. I was very pleased to have this opportunity to go to another country and enjoy the adventure. In the past my family had never traveled. I only remember short trips my father and I took to Warsaw when he went on business to buy leather for his customers' shoes and boots.

Chapter VII

Denmark: 1947

E ARLY IN THE MORNING, Wanda and Jurek took me to the seaport of Gdansk. There we met the Polish ship Batory. There were
hundreds of children from Poland and other European nations. We all
boarded and stood on the deck to wave good-bye to relatives waiting
below. I had never been on such a big boat before; it was just like a city.
We were shown to our cabins by the steward and followed him down
to the lower deck with our suitcases. I shared a cabin with Suzanna,
a young girl from Hungary. Although Suzanna did not speak Polish
and I did not speak Hungarian, we managed to communicate with our
hands and facial expressions. She was a pretty blonde with long braids,
while I was a brunette with long hair in ringlets, hanging down my
shoulders past my waist.

The crossing from Gdansk to Denmark was a lot of fun. I met
many boys and girls from various European countries, most of them
friendly and outgoing. What a treat to eat everything I wanted—and
in abundance. At dinner time, the captain of the ship came over to visit
with us. He asked many questions about our backgrounds. We became
good friends. He told me about his wife back home and he wanted me
to meet her. The captain gave me his address and I corresponded with
him and his wife for some time, exchanging letters and pictures.

When we arrived in Denmark, we were met by our respective Danish families. My family's name was Larsen. The Larsens lived on Fynn
Island, on a small farm with their daughter, Vibeke; their son Erik was
away in the navy. The Larsens had a dog named Lady, a large, gentle

dog; years later, when I watched Lassie on television, she reminded me of Lady. Lady and I became good friends.

Vibeke was about my age and she tried to make me feel comfortable in their home. The only problem was the language barrier. The Larsens did not speak Polish and I did not speak Danish. We had a small Polish-Danish phrase book, but I was a foolish and obstinate teenager at the time, and resistant to learning the Danish language. The only word that I still remember is *Toomadewige* meaning, "Don't touch."

The family was very good to me and showed me a nice time. There were other Danish host families with Polish youngsters, and the Larsens made sure that I had contact with the other Polish boys and girls periodically so we could get together.

The family's abundance of food made quite an impression on me. What stands out in my mind is the large larder full of cheeses, hams and bacon. The meals were incredible! Every morning at seven, the family would start off with Danish pastry and a beverage. At 9 A.M., they came in from the fields and put out a spread of eggs, bacon and dozens of cheeses, the freshest and tastiest cheeses that I have ever had.

The lunches and dinners were equally lavish and plentiful. When the family returned home before dinner, they would milk the cows. Their barn was always spotless, very modern looking. The cows were milked electronically. I was fortunate to hand-milk a cow on several occasions and drank the warm, fresh milk directly from the cow—an incredible experience. The milk was rich and absolutely delicious.

The Larsens were farmers and worked in the fields all day. Vibeke and I liked to play. We cut out paper dolls of the Danish royal family, and enjoyed dressing the dolls in their elegant royal gowns. The Larsens had a car; however, most Danes used bicycles for transportation. In those days, one saw hundreds of bicycles in the city streets as well as in the country.

The second day of my visit, Vibeke invited me to ride into town on a bicycle that the family got for me. I was not experienced on a bicycle; however, I was willing to learn. Both of us mounted our bicycles and I followed Vibeke. We went down a fairly steep, long hill, going quite fast and carefree. All of a sudden I hit a fence at the bottom of the hill and fell head over heels, smashing the front of the wheel into the fence. I wasn't hurt, but the bicycle, of course, had to be repaired. From then on I pedaled more cautiously and there were many more rides without accidents.

The Larsens were a close-knit family. They spent much of their time at home, except for marketing trips to the city, and church on Sundays. Sometimes we went to birthday parties in other Danish host families' homes and met children from other European countries. Most of the Danish families were very generous and kind to me. One of our outings consisted of a trip to Odense, the birthplace of Hans Christian Anderson; it was fun to visit a new place.

Vibeke and I took long walks with Lady or sat in the garden, reading. I was given a diary for my trip and faithfully recorded all the events of the days, especially new experiences. At age 11, I was a big letter-writer and corresponded with people that I had met along the way. I wrote to Wanda and Jurek almost daily.

When it was time to leave Denmark and return to Poland, the Larsen family helped me pack my belongings. I had much more to take home than what I came with. Afterwards, I took the train back to Copenhagen to board the Batory for our return trip. We spent a short time in Copenhagen and enjoyed a view of the city. The captain greeted me warmly; we were now good friends. He wanted to know all about my visit and let me know that he told his wife Margereta about me and that she wanted to meet me.

The passage back to Gdansk was a little quieter. We had left our good friends behind and were returning to our families. It had been a marvelous vacation and an experience not to be forgotten. The cultural interaction between the Danes and the children from other European countries was invaluable. I was sad to leave the Larsens, but I was fatter and richer in memories. It was time to return to Bydogscsz, to be with Wanda and Jurek.

CHAPTER VIII

❧ *Back in Bydogoszcz: 1947*

W HEN I ARRIVED in Gdansk, Wanda and Jurek were waiting for me. We talked all the way back to Bydgoszcz. They wanted to know everything—about the people I stayed with and the things we did. I had plenty to talk about, the Larsen family and all the new friends I made in Denmark.

I arrived on a Saturday afternoon and the following day we all went to church together. Wanda and Jurek were devout Catholics and I worshipped with them every Sunday. Shortly after we moved to Bydgoszcz, I started to study the catechism to prepare for my first communion.

Wanda sent me to a convent every Wednesday afternoon where the nuns taught me about Catholicism. Although Wanda and Jurek never forced me to worship in their faith, I had a very strong need to belong to a church and pray to God. The religion was extremely important to me. It gave me strength to go on and hope that one day I might find my family of birth. I was a very good Catholic; I obeyed my family and God, and went to confession once a week to atone for my wrongdoings.

I studied the catechism for several months until it was time to take my first communion, the first week in June. Wanda's mother made me a beautiful white dress. I wore a white bow in my hair, and Wanda bought me pretty white shoes and socks. If I do say so myself, I looked angelic in this pure white ensemble. I was very proud of this accomplishment; I felt a real sense of belonging to the church and now I was able to partake in the communion ceremony during the Sunday services.

When things went wrong for me, I always knew that I could get down on my knees in front of a portrait of Jesus Christ or the Madonna and pray very hard until my worries vanished. It was amazing how much better I felt after praying. I found the Catholic religion to be a very comforting faith; if one truly believes in the doctrine, it can be very soothing and life is less stressful.

Following my return to Bydgoszcz, I started the eighth grade. My friend Basia was still living with her aunt and we were very happy to see each other. Basia was excited to hear about my adventures in Denmark. I was asked to give a speech to my class about my trip.

All this time, I never gave up hope and continued to search for my real family. I had some recollection of an uncle named Abraham living in Paris, France. He was a younger brother of my father and when I was a little girl in Poland, he used to visit us with his wife Gittel. I also remember the many presents he brought us when he visited Okuniew. Before going to Denmark, I had written to my uncle and, to my amazement, I heard back from him. He wrote that he wanted me to come to Paris to live with him and his common-law wife Edzia and Edzia's daughter Helene, who was about my age. My uncle was in his late 40's at the time. To bring me to Paris, he had to seek permission from the French government, which entailed much red tape and paperwork.

When I returned from Denmark, a letter arrived from my uncle. In the letter, he tried to reassure me to be patient that he was still waiting for a reply from the French government to enable me to emigrate from Poland to France. I was very anxious to go to France, so it was hard for me to be patient. I wanted very much to be with my own family—the little family that I had left was very precious to me.

Shortly after I received the letter from my uncle, two tall men in dark suits arrived at our apartment, telling me that I was to leave for Paris in two days to be reunited with my uncle. I had a hard time comprehending the news, and I had only one day to get ready, to pack and say goodbye to my family and my best friend Basia. Wanda and I were both confused, not fully comprehending the meaning of all this.

I was frantic. I ran to Basia's house to tell her the news and she became hysterical; we were both crying and hugging each other with broken hearts. The prospect of separation was devastating for both of us. I tried to reassure Basia that we would keep in touch and visit each other soon.

It was also sad for me to leave Wanda and Jurek, who had been my family for the past five years. They had saved my life; they were the family that had stuck by my side.

When the two men returned the following day, I was packed and ready to go physically, but emotionally, I was teary-eyed from my goodbyes. This was a big milestone. I was leaving behind the sad memories of the loss of my family in Poland, and beginning a new life. The unknown was very scary.

Family picture in honor of Anna's Bat Mitzvah, November 1, 2008.
FRONT ROW (LEFT TO RIGHT): *Lindsey, Anna, Maria,*
Zachary, Jack, Michelle, Laura, Alex.
BACK ROW: *Glen, Lauren, Ken, Isabel, Scott.*

*Maria's paternal grandparents, Ester and Eshraim Okuniew,
Poland, before WWII.*

*Abraham and Gitl Polanowicz,
Maria's aunt and uncle.*

Aunts and uncles in Poland prior to WWII.

Maria's aunts and an uncle with Maria's youner brother Josef (front) and oldest sister Micha (right). No one survived the war.

Maria's oldest brother Moshe (center) with his two aunts.

Maria and friend in Okuniew after Maria's escape from the Warsaw Ghetto, 1943.

Map of Poland (2008).
My journey shown in red dotted line.

THE WARSAW GHETTO

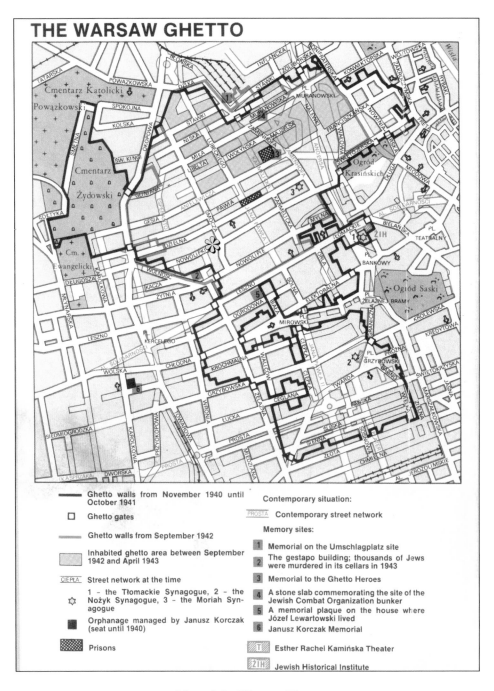

Map of the Warsaw Ghetto.
My street is marked with a yellow asterisk.

LEFT: Wanda (left) and her mother-in-law, Mrs. Hadrysiak Maria in front, age 9, Poland 1944.

BELOW: Abraham Polanowicz (center) with two Czech inmates from Auschwitz. All three escaped before liberation.

My wedding portrait,
December 20, 1958..

fluently by this time." She stayed there throughout the war, until rescuers working for a Jewish agency found her. She still corresponds with members of her surrogate family in Warsaw.

But she never discovered

Above, Maria Segal as a child in Poland; right, Segal today.

memories of events they didn't understand. Some didn't know until adulthood that they were Jewish.

All are Jewish children who survived the Holocaust by liv-

ABOVE: Arizona Republic *article. Picture on left is from Pornichet, France in 1949.*

BELOW:

Laura (11/7/1961), Glen (4/4/1963), Michelle (3/25/1960).

*Maria and husband David with their three children, Glen,
Michelle, and Laura. Scottsdale, Arizona, 1988.*

Maria hiking in the Grand Canyon, hiking was Maria's favorite hobby, 1986.

Michelle, Laura, Maria and Glen after crossing the Mexican border with our pottery, Arizona.

Maria graduates with a Masters in Social Work, Bernie (dog), Arizona State University 1977.

LEFT: Michelle's graduation from Whitman College, 1982.

BELOW LEFT: Glen's graduation from Whitman College, 1985.

BELOW RIGHT: Laura's graduation from UCLA School of Law, 1986.

*RIGHT: Michelle Segal marries
Scott Greer September 25, 1982.*

*CENTER: Laura Segal marries
Ken Stovitz, December 19, 1992.*

*BELOW: Glen Segal marries
Lauren, August 31, 1996.*

Anna Stovitz (age 5) and
Jack Stovitz (age 2).

Isabel Greer (age 5) dancing.

Alex, Michelle and Isabel Greer.

Maria, Glen, Michelle and Laura Breckenridge, Colorado 2000.

*Maria retires from her life as a social worker
at Arizona State, DES, June 15th, 2000.*

LEFT: Maria with cousin, Maurice Najman, Paris 1988

BELOW: Maria and Uncle Abraham, Paris, 1988

Laura Stovitz, Abraham Polanowicz, Maria and Edzia Fontainbleu, France 1996.

31 August 1998

Maria Segal
7861 Via Costa
Scottsdale, AZ 85258

Dear Ms. Segal,

Thank you for contributing your testimony to Survivors of the Shoah Visual History Foundation. In sharing your story, you have granted future generations the opportunity to experience a direct connection with history.

Your interview will be carefully preserved as an important part of the most comprehensive library of Holocaust testimonies ever assembled. Far into the future, people will be able to see a face, hear a voice, and observe a life, so that they may listen and learn, and always remember.

Thank you for your invaluable contribution, your strength, and your generosity of spirit.

All my best,

Steven Spielberg
Chairman

Letter from Steven Spielberg, Aug. 31st 1998.

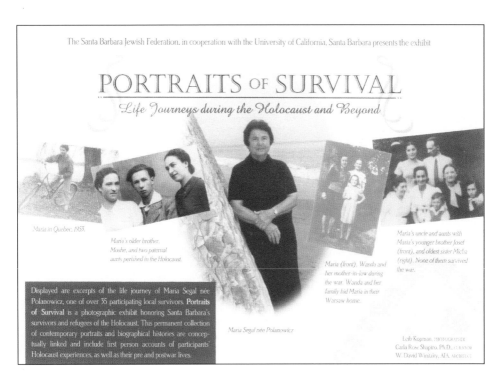

Portraits of Survival, November 19th, 2003.

Opening of Portraits of Survival .
BACK ROW: *Scott, Ken, Laura, Maria, Michelle, Isabel, Lauren,*
Lindsey (camera shy) and Glen. FRONT ROW: *Anna, Jack, Zachy, and Alex.*

Portraits of Survival

EXHIBIT HOURS: MON – THURS, 10 AM - 5 PM; FRI, 9 AM - 4 PM

FOR INFO OR DOCENT-LED GROUP TOURS: SHANA AIRES, (805) 957-1115, EXT. 123

FOR FUNDING OPPORTUNITIES: DAVID HARRIS, (805) 957-1115, EXT. 106.

Funding provided by UCSB, Santa Barbara Bank & Trust, the Karuna Foundation, and generous donors.

"VIDEO *PORTRAITS*"

The DVD of "Video *Portraits of Survival*" will soon be available for purchase. Visit www.portraitsofsurvival.org or call for more info. The film will also be released to television stations. Production of a second "Video *Portraits*" is in progress, supported in part by funds granted by **Chancellor Henry Yang** to the UCSB Department of Film Studies.

THOUSANDS OF VISITORS!

Summer tours included students from **Villa Esperanza**, an alternative school for students in the juvenile courts system; **Salvation Army Men's Adult Rehabilitation Center** *(pictured above)*; and a diverse group that included a Bar Mitzvah boy, his grandmother and sponsor, Federation board members and their families, a new visitor who just discovered his Jewish roots and two German journalists touring Santa Barbara *(pictured below)*.

Second Generation (Children of Survivors) Book and Film Discussion Group
Accepting new members
2nd Thurs. of the month > 4 – 5:30 pm
RSVP AND INFO: (805) 957-1116, EXT. 119

Docent Training and Refresher
For both experienced and new docents
Thursday, October 19 > 10 am – noon
✿ Share your experiences as a docent and refresh your expertise
✿ Meet with other participants in the *Portraits of Survival* programs
✿ Learn how best to present your story and serve as a docent for future programs
If you are a survivor or child of a survivor, your story is a precious gift to our community. Consider becoming a docent. ADVANCED REGISTRATION NECESSARY.
CONTACT PROGRAM DIRECTOR DR. ELIZABETH WOLFSON FOR MORE INFO AND TO RSVP.

"Neighbors Who Disappeared"
An Exhibition on the Holocaust by students from the Czech Republic
Presented by Temple Beth El & Calvary Chapel
October 9 – 31
Temple Beth El in Santa Maria
FOR HOURS AND LOCATION:
KENNETHLWOLF@MSN.COM, (805) 260-3113

A VERY SPECIAL THANK YOU...

To docents who helped coordinate tours this summer: **Carole Fox**, **Cecia Hess**, **Julie Jeffreys**, **Barbara Marx**, and **Laura Smith**.

To our dedicated docent-speakers for this summer's tours: **Helga Carden**, **Renee Clement**, **Fred Jamner**, **Erika Kahn**, **Stan Ostern**, **Katy Renner**, **Maria Segal**, and **Margaret Singer**.

We could not do it without you!

Now accepting reservations for tours. Transportation for schools can be arranged. Contact Shana Aires, (805) 957-1115, ext. 123.

Newsletter, Portraits of Survival activities.

Sara DeArmond

Jimmy Raack
It was a real eye-opening
experience Thank you for
sharing the stories with us.

Thank you very much for
every thing that you did
for our class. It was a
wonderful experience for
me. Chelsea Winkelmeyer

thanks for sharing
your stories, I learned
a lot.
Sasil Nali

this was a fantastic
and intense experience.
I really enjoyed it.
Thanks so much!
~Masha Mogonova

thank you so much. It was
a truely incredibly experience.
I wish we could have had
more time! I hope to get
the chance all at the Santa Barbara Jewish Federation
to come and see (with special gratitude to Elizabeth Wolfson, Ruth Steinberg,
the rest of Carol Fox, and the docents — Katy, Ann, Barbara, Helga,
the exhibit. Thank you again... and Margaret) —
Veronica Pessino

THANK YOU,
JESSIE LONG
It was very
fulfilling!
—Peera Sukavivatone

Thank you for providing
such a wonderful exhibit.
The stories were very moving,
and it makes me appreciate
our freedom even more.
—Natalie Ridling

Thank you so much for
Thank you your stories and
experiences.
Joe Faulkner

Thank You

Thank you so much for the survivors,
so much for presentation
telling your stories
to us. I really
enjoyed them.
—Kira Adams

Thank You for sharing
this with us. I know a little
more of what actually happened.
Thank you so much! December 14, 2004
♡ Kaitlyn Ekell

Thank you so much for
broadening and deepening our understanding
experience. the emotional

Cecily Stewart
Thank you
so much for
taking time to share
your stories with us.
They inspired me
to love those who
nobody else loves.
You are all very
amazing!
♥Roya Bazaz

Thank you for
your enlightening
lecture and exhibit
It has been an
honor to learn
more about the
Jewish people's history,

Thank you! These stories were
very insightful & I am
glad to have come.
—Eric Wilder

Jesse Elconin   Thank you for your presence
—Jonathen Suddon

Thanks for
sharing your
excellent stories
with us,

SAN MARCOS HIGH SCHOOL
STUDENT'S FEEDBACK

We thank you for a well-planned, moving
experience with you. The exhibit is a powerful
presentation of so many, varied Survivor Stories.
The photos and narratives humanize the history we're
studying in class, and the docent testimonials
bring even greater personal meaning to us. Thank
you for helping us understand how close to the
surface these memories/histories are. Hearing these
individual accounts in conjunction with the exhibit
and our class studies is a precious gift, and we are
grateful for this opportunity to learn from and
remember with you. Sincerely,

San Marcos HS, speaking to students about Holocaust experiences.

Thank-you card from the children of Laguna Blanca School.

Wanda and Maria at Wanda's sons house, Bydgoszcz 2007.

Wanda, Agnieszka, Maria and Mariola, near Turon, June 2007.

Maria and a student in front of the monument at Majdanek Concentration Camp.

Burned ashes of victims, Majdanek, May 2007.

RIGHT: Maria inside the school, Bydgoszcz, Poland 2007.

BELOW: Wanda and Maria at Maria's school in Bydgoszcz, Poland, June 2007.

Front: Wanda, Maria, Agnieszka. Back: Manolia, Jurek, Ryszu, and Tomek.

Israeli Embassy and Polisz officials. Wanda & Maria with flowers and awards in Bydgoszcz, Polland, August 10th, 2008.

Photo: Ross Payson

"12810," sculpture by Izzy Greer.

Years after its reopening as a museum, Auschwitz still has not won back its humanity: these were the same gates, the same walls that witnessed the horrors of the past. My family and I traveled to Auschwitz armed with the name and a picture of Abraham Polanowicz given to me by my grandma, Maria Segal, his niece. Through the foreboding gates in one of the uniform brick buildings amidst lightly falling rain in the back corner of the left room was a white three ring binder. There were no embellishments or decorations: this binder had a solemn purpose, to reconnect those people once broken. We flipped to the P's, and we found him: Abraham Polanowicz, 12810. He had escaped Auschwitz along with two Czech prisoners, and along with my grandma survived the Holocaust. It was this experience combined with the goodness of my grandma that provided the inspiration for this sculpture: of a caged figure emerging from formlessness and breaking free from cage and chains.

—Izzy Greer

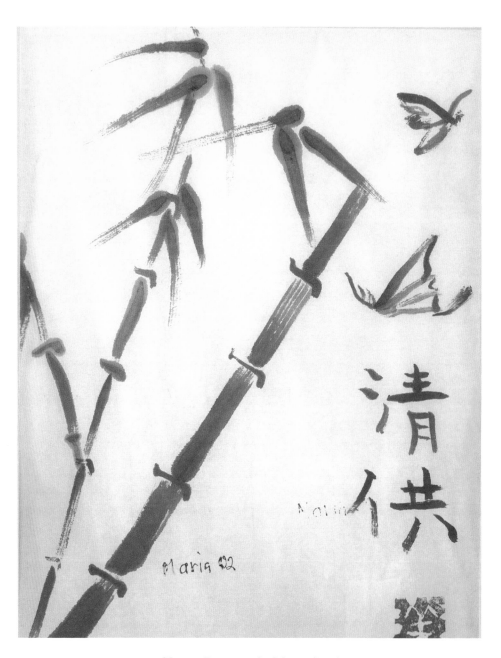

Chinese Print art by Maria Segal.

CHAPTER IX

❧ *Paris: 1948*

ALL THE JEWISH CHILDREN from Poland were housed in a suburb of Warsaw for several days prior to going to Paris. We were given false papers to enable us to cross the German-French border. While we were waiting to depart for France with hundreds of other Jewish boys and girls who had survived the war, there was little for us to do.

I met a girl named Natasia; she too was an orphan with a similar background to mine. Natasia also lived with a Catholic family and attended church on a regular basis, like I did. Here, everyone was Jewish and it was hard for some of the staff to understand our need to go to church and attend mass. Natasia and I cried on each others' shoulders and spoke about our natural families, and of the families who saved our lives. It was very therapeutic to find someone who understood. Finally, the day arrived when we boarded the trains with our pouches to hold our fake passports.

Just before boarding the train we were told that our destination was Israel with a stopover in Paris. "Well," I told everyone, "I am not going to Israel. I am going to Paris; my uncle is expecting me."

The train ride was long and tiring. We arrived, cleaned up and had dinner, then went upstairs to get ready for bed. I asked one of the counselors if my uncle would be coming to get me and his reply was, "You do not have an uncle." I was devastated and realized that I had been deceived while still in Poland. I felt desperate. Suddenly, I had an idea. I wrote a note to my uncle and begged one of the waitresses at dinner to deliver it to him, telling her that it was very important that he get it right away.

The next day we were told to pack and bring our suitcases to the waiting bus. I refused to take my luggage to the bus, but they dragged me; then I refused to put my suitcase on the bus.

At midnight, my uncle Abraham arrived at the gate. The security people refused to let him in. He got extremely angry and told them that I was his only living relative and that he had been a prisoner in Auschwitz. After much arguing, he succeeded in getting me out before the group left for Israel. It was quite a victory to be free again. Needless to say, I was very happy to see my uncle.

Uncle Abraham and I got along just fine; my cousin Helene was also nice to me and we had a good time together. Edzia, his common-law wife, was an entirely different story. By this time, I was quite independent, with a mind of my own. The most important thing for me during this period of my life was to continue to go to church and practice the Catholic religion. This did not sit well with Aunt Edzia. She told me that I could not go to church as long as I lived with her and Uncle Abraham.

I had only been with my relatives a few days when I realized that living in this situation would not work for me. I decided to go to the kiosk down the street and buy a Polish newspaper. I found out the name of the editor of this paper and went to see him: Mr. Marymont. I explained to him my need to go to church and, as a Catholic himself, he understood. He offered to take me home with him to his wife and his two young children. I spent the weekend with the Marymonts and Monday morning we drove back to Paris. He put me under the care of two young women who worked for him.

Mr. Marymont came up with the idea of enrolling me in a Polish boarding school in Paris. While he made the arrangements, his two young women employees entertained me, taking me to the zoo, to shows, sightseeing, and out to eat. By the end of the week, I was in school.

I had a cousin in Paris, Maurice, and his wife Marie. They were very good to me and I visited them quite often. Maurice had known Abraham for many years and was on good terms with him, but not with Edzia. Maurice told me that my uncle was very sad that I had run away from his house. Later on I met with Abraham or he would visit me when I went to visit Marie and Maurice. I had little to do with Edzia, however. Most of my time was spent with Marie and Maurice and other acquaintances of my parents from Poland, Dorka and Itzak. Dorka and Itzak entertained a lot on weekends. They usually invited Maurice, Marie, Abraham and me. I liked going there; they had a pretty house with a large garden in the backyard—and Dorka was a wonderful cook. We all sat outside talking and enjoying the delicious food that Dorka prepared. Of course, there was always wine to complement the meal.

I loved the boarding school. All the classes were in Polish, and on Sunday I could go to church and no one would try to prevent me. I learned a great deal, and the classes were small. We went to museums, the theater and even the opera. I remember that my very first opera at the Paris Opera House was "Boris Godounov" followed by "Faust." Our class got all dressed up in our finest clothes for the opera. I was amazed by the beauty of the building—so many elaborate paintings, carvings and exquisite chandeliers. I was fortunate to be exposed to perhaps the best culture in the world. No matter how many times I went to the Louvre, there was always more to see, and each trip meant another new discovery of wonder. Even when I went back to the Louvre years later, I was still in awe of this marvelous rich collection that represented the cradle of our civilization. Paris has great beauty and is rich in its abundance of churches, museums, gardens and fascinating buildings and bridges on the River Seine.

While at boarding school, I became friendly with my Latin teacher, Mrs. Spanow. Mrs. Spanow invited me to her home on weekends where I became acquainted with her husband and son. The Spanows came from Poland after the war. Dr. Spanow was not able to practice medicine in France until he took his medical boards in French, so he worked in a hospital. The family decided to seek their opportunity in Australia and made plans to leave France shortly after school was out. I was very sorry to see them leave Paris.

Prior to their departure to Australia, Mrs. Spanow introduced me to a Jewish couple from Montreal, Canada. They wanted to adopt a young orphan without any family attachments. The Spanows talked to me about this couple and suggested that I meet with them. I agreed to meet them, but I decided that I was not interested in being adopted. Because they wanted a child without any family, I would have to give up my relationship with my uncle. It was a good idea, but not for me. I was not willing to give up my relationship with my uncle, who was the only family I had left.

There was another couple in Paris I made friends with who were also childless and wanted to adopt me. Nonetheless, I had made up my mind that I was too old to be adopted and not interested in committing to a family. The idea of going to Canada, however, was appealing.

The Spanows helped me make contact with the Canadian Jewish Joint Committee who sponsored young Jewish children and helped them immigrate to Canada. The process took several months of waiting and filling out papers.

Dorka and Itzak invited me to stay with them while I waited to immigrate to Canada. I finished boarding school and since it was summertime, Dorka helped me apply through a Jewish organization to attend summer camp. I had never been to camp before; this was another new experience for me. I was with Jewish boys and girls and shared in the same activities. By this time, I had learned a little French, because I had attended a French school for a few months. The camp was lots of fun. We went on day hikes, swimming, had arts and crafts and other group activities. I became interested in art and often preferred to sketch alone. I also had a French boyfriend named Bernard; he was very cute and we had fun spending time together.

When I returned to Paris, my paperwork was still not ready, so I decided to go to school at a residential facility for homeless Jewish war victims, an orphanage, in Livry Gargan, a suburb of Paris. I picked up the French language rapidly. We had a physical education program every week on Thursdays, because the French do not go to school on Thursdays. We did a lot of gymnastics; I really liked gymnastics and sports in general. I played the position of goalie on the soccer team. We were invited to perform a gymnastics show for a local organization and since I was the smallest and lightest, I was always put on top of the pyramids. I was not afraid at all to be on the tip-top of the pyramid and enjoyed showing off my bravery.

I also liked to memorize and recite poetry. On one occasion, I was asked to recite a poem at a big Polish festival in Paris. As I was quite adept at memorizing, I was given two days to learn the poem by heart and get ready to recite to a large audience. The day of the recital, I got stage fright when I found out how large the concert hall was that I would perform in. When we arrived there, I became even more nervous, seeing lots of people and bright lights. They assured me that another student would be behind the curtain with the book to prompt me in case I forgot the lines.

When I went on stage, the glare of the lights appeared to block everything out, and butterflies in my stomach were fluttering away. However, I went on anyway and began to recite. All went well. When I finished and went behind the curtain, the girl with the book told me that she was sorry but she had lost the page to my poem. I felt like saying, "Thanks for nothing." But I was glad I had remembered my lines anyway.

While waiting to immigrate to Canada, I went back to live with Dorka and Itzak. I loved to read books until wee hours of the morning, and sleep until noon. I did not have any responsibilities—no school, no work, just an occasional visit to the Canadian Jewish Congress regarding my immigration papers.

In the meantime, I maintained contact with my uncle and my cousins, and saw them as often as I was able. Abraham was not happy about my going to Canada; he would have preferred that I remain in Paris so he could see me more often. I could not be persuaded at this point; my mind was made up. I wanted to seek out a new life for myself—new adventures, new countries, new people and new opportunities.

CHAPTER X

ᴄᴡ *Canada: 1950*

AFTER ALL THE WAITING, the day finally came for me to leave
Paris, my relatives and friends. Dorka made a big going-away
party for me. She invited my uncle, aunt, cousins, her relatives and
friends. Everyone asked me lots of questions. Of course, I did not
have any answers about where I was going, or with whom I would live
in Canada. I had been told that I would go to Montreal and would
meet with my social worker who would make the arrangements for
me to live with a family. Gretta Fisher was my assigned social worker
in Canada.

Everyone at the party brought me gifts. We said our goodbyes, and
hugged and kissed when the party was over. The French love to kiss
twice on each cheek, whether one is related or not.

The day of my departure, Uncle Abraham, my cousins and Dorka
came to the train station to see me off. I left Le Havre for England,
where I would board a large ship for Canada.

We sailed on the Cunard Line, on a ship that was even bigger
than the Batory that I had sailed on to Denmark. I met a group of
young French women and men who were also sailing to Canada. We
sat together at the same dining room table and enjoyed socializing on
the ship's deck. It was fun. We were aboard the ship on July 14, 1950—
Bastille Day. We had a great time singing French songs, dancing and
eating French specialties that the cook prepared for us.

One evening, I informed the waiter at dinner that it was Claude's
birthday, one of the young men at the table. The waiter promised to
keep it a secret and bring a birthday cake for Claude.

We all gathered at the table, tasting the many delicious courses and chatting as usual. When it was time for dessert, the waiter arrived with a beautiful chocolate cake that said, "Happy Birthday, Claude!" All of us sang "Happy Birthday," to Claude's great amazement and bewilderment. Of course, it was not Claude's birthday—it was just a joke and everyone had a wonderful time laughing along.

The five days of crossing the Atlantic went very rapidly. When we arrived at the seaport in Quebec City, a group of Jewish women from Hadassah greeted us with refreshments. One of the women, Mrs. Goldberg, came over to me and asked all sorts of personal questions. Mrs. Goldberg went on to invite me to live with her, her husband and daughter Audrey, who was about my age. The invitation was appealing to me, but as I explained to her, I was on my way to Montreal to meet my social worker, Gretta Fisher. Mrs. Goldberg gave me her telephone number and told me that she wanted Gretta to call her.

I arrived in Montreal in the evening, quite tired from the journey on the boat and train. Gretta was at the station to greet me. She was a tall, stately woman in her thirties with a very warm and gentle smile. Gretta had a family lined up for me to stay with; however, because it was so late, she took me to her apartment for the night and would bring me over to the Elkin family the following morning. Gretta was fluent in French so we communicated well. I told Gretta about my meeting with Mrs. Goldberg in Quebec City and her intentions. Gretta promised to call her after she got me settled with the Elkins.

I spent a pleasant evening with Gretta, telling her all about my passage on the ship, my French friends that I had met, and all the relatives who had come to see me off at the Gare du Nord train station in Paris.

When I woke the next morning in this strange city, I was lonely for Paris and the people with whom I was close. Gretta made breakfast for me—not like the breakfasts I was used to in Paris. A Canadian breakfast is very different from the French breakfast. I faced a new country, new people and a new set of customs in life style and eating habits. For a 15-year-old girl, it took a great deal of getting used to all the changes. Gretta drove me to the Elkin house with all my worldly possessions in a suitcase and a fishnet with gifts from my relatives in Paris.

Mrs. Elkin, a friendly, warm-hearted lady, received me with open arms. The Elkins had three girls ranging in age from two to seven. I shared a room with the Elkins' seven-year-old-daughter. My stay with them was temporary, until Gretta was able to find a more permanent home for me. Meanwhile, Gretta promised to call Mrs. Goldberg in Quebec City to explore my placement there.

I spent two weeks with the Elkins. They were kind people and allowed me to visit my French friends, whom I had met on the ship. One of the young men, Jean, was very attentive to me. He picked me up and took me sightseeing all over Montreal. Jean had a friend who was an intern at Hotel Dieu Hospital, an old building still run by Catholic nuns. Jean took me there to meet his friends. Hotel Dieu is one of the oldest hospitals in Canada and very interesting. I saw Jean quite a few times, but I got messages from the Elkins that perhaps Jean was too old for me to cultivate that relationship.

Two weeks went by and Gretta called to let me know that she had spoken with Mrs. Goldberg; the family wanted me to come to Quebec City to live with them. Their children had married, except for one 15-year-old daughter, Trudy, who still lived at home. Gretta told me that she would make arrangements for us to go to Quebec City by train the following week, about a four-hour ride.

I had some apprehensions about going to live with a family I knew so little about. Gretta reassured me that everything would work out for the best, and in the event that I did not like living in Quebec City with the Goldberg family, I could call her and she would try to find a different family for me to live with in Montreal.

Chapter XI

❧ Quebec City: 1950

Gretta and I were met at the train station by Mrs. Goldberg, who took us to her home in the suburbs of Quebec City. Her daughter Trudy was sitting in the living room waiting for us. Trudy was a tall teenager, quite attractive with long blonde hair.

Gretta and I were shown the three-bedroom home, tastefully furnished and very comfortable, including the room that Trudy and I would share. I got the feeling that Trudy was reluctant about sharing her room with me, and possibly not happy with the living arrangements her mother had made. I said goodbye to Gretta with some apprehension.

The next day, Mrs. Goldberg took me to register for the semester at Quebec High School. I picked out the classes I knew I would enjoy. When I arrived in Canada, I spoke French, Polish, and some Yiddish from my childhood in Okuniew. Of course, I did not speak any English and so I had to learn the English language to be able to communicate with other students and teachers. At first, the learning process was a real challenge, and I did not do well because of my limited comprehension. As time went on, I had a better understanding of the language and did better on my tests.

In time I started to socialize with the students I had met through Trudy. Quebec City had a definite class division. The middle and upper class students socialized amongst themselves. Around the Christmas holidays in particular, there were many parties. I was invited to all the parties because of Trudy. I even dated a young man from my class, Bill.

As I have written, the Catholic Church and attending mass were very important to me after my time with Wanda. However, while living with the Goldbergs in Quebec City, I did not go to church. I knew the Goldbergs would not approve of a Jewish girl going to church. In fact, they did not know at all that I had embraced the Catholic faith while living with Wanda in Poland. I kept hidden the picture of my first communion in my beautiful white dress.

When I was leaving Bydgoszcz, Wanda had given me a copy of a beautifully bound book called *Pan Tadeusz*, by Adam Mickiewicz, a well known author of Polish literature. I had pasted the picture of my first communion between two pages in front of the hard cover. I had the book with me in Canada, but no one ever knew about the picture, except for me.

As time went on, I was sad at not being able to attend mass on Sunday. Shortly after I settled in with the Goldberg family, the Jewish High Holidays were approaching. Mrs. Goldberg had some used clothes from her two older daughters which she took to a dressmaker to alter for me, so I could wear them to synagogue. The clothes were not exactly my taste, but I agreed to wear them. I remember them to this day: brownish beige tweed suits that I did not care for.

The holidays arrived and Mrs. Goldberg prepared some festive Jewish dishes. I enjoyed the holiday food but, to be honest, I was bored with the services. Not being able to read Hebrew or understand the prayers made it very unpleasant for me. We went to Kol Nidre, the service preceding the day of Yom Kippur. This is the holiest holiday in the Jewish religion. The chanting on Kol Nidre is very moving. When I heard the music that evening, it penetrated deep into my heart and made me very sad. It brought back memories from my childhood, from the past, my family and all the religious experiences when I lived with my parents and my siblings. I had been a very young child when I lived in Okuniew, barely five when Hitler invaded Poland.

This was the big turning point in my life: I had to choose between Catholicism and Judaism. Deep in my heart, I had a longing for my roots, my heritage, and a feeling that I belonged to the Jewish people. My connection to the Catholic Church completely changed. I knew that I could no longer betray my parents, my grandparents, my sisters, my brothers and relatives. From this moment on, I stopped going to church. I no longer had the need to worship in the Catholic Church. I knew deep in my heart that I belonged to the Jewish people. I have never shared these experiences with anyone. Although I currently do not attend synagogue on a regular basis, it is important to me to recapture my past and honor where I come from.

Eventually, it became clear that Trudy was not happy with my presence in her home. She resented the competition and wanted to be the only one getting all the attention from her parents and friends. Very often she would tell me, "Don't touch the night stand or the lamp. This is my room." Mrs. Goldberg did not know what was going on between us, and I did not want to tell her because I thought it would hurt her feelings. It became increasingly more difficult for me to tolerate Trudy's mood swings. Finally it got to the point that I had to tell Ms. Fisher, my social worker. Ms. Fisher suggested that I move back to Montreal; she was willing to find me a family.

One day, Ms. Fisher arrived by train and came to the Goldbergs' residence. We decided it was time to discuss the tension between Trudy and me. Ms. Fisher explained that living with the family was not working out for me because of that, and that she had found another family for me to live with. We left together for Montreal with all my belongings.

In Montreal, I lived with the Lerner family as a boarder, free to come and go. Shirley Lerner was a very talented musician and taught me to play the piano, which I enjoyed. During the day I attended Montreal High School for Girls. By this time my English was much better and improved each day. It was still difficult for me to understand colloquial expressions and jokes. When everyone laughed after a joke was told, I just looked at them and smiled. In Montreal I made many friends and, thanks to Gretta, I had many invitations on the weekends.

When the time came for matriculation from high school, I was not sure I would be able to understand the questions. When I discussed this with my teacher, she was able to get me permission from the Board of Examiners to use a Polish-English dictionary to facilitate the translation of questions on the examination. I passed the exams and decided to go to McDonald College, a teachers' college in St. Anne de Bellevue, in the Province of Quebec, and lived in a dorm. My roommate was Irene, an acquaintance from high school. We were both enrolled in the teaching program. Irene and I had a good time at McDonald. I remember our class in psychology. When we came back to our room, we looked at the questions on our handout and we appeared to have all the symptoms stated on the paper.

St. Anne de Bellevue was a small town within walking distance from the college. At times we went to town for food, shopping or an occasional movie. Some weekends I went to Montreal to visit my friends. I attended McDonald College for two years and obtained a certificate to teach up to the eighth grade. I was 18 years old.

I decided I wanted to teach young children, and for four years I taught second grade. My first school was on the outskirts of Montreal. I had a second grade class with a racially diverse population. I loved teaching the seven-year-olds; they are totally devoted to the teacher. We had good times together. Because the class was interracial, we had some interesting discussions in our social studies classes. I always liked art and so we had painting sessions in our classroom every Friday. At times the parents invited me for lunch and tea, which gave me a better insight into family dynamics. I really enjoyed the youngsters and had a very good time teaching.

The following year, I taught in a school a little closer to the town I lived in. In contrast to my first school, the students here were predominantly Caucasian. Later I taught in a suburb and was able to take a bus across the street from my apartment. I shared the apartment with Peggy, a fine person whom I knew from high school. We got along very well. She was dating a charming young man from Ireland named Doug. Doug visited our apartment often and eventually he and Peggy married and moved to their own apartment.

Although I was happy teaching, I was not totally satisfied with only two years of college, so I decided to enroll in college to get my Bachelor of Arts degree. I went to St. George William University at night and during the summer, and taught school during the day. After I got my degree, I continued to teach elementary school children, which I enjoyed best.

❧A New Beginning

I MET MY HUSBAND David while vacationing in the Adirondacks at Scaroon Manor. David and I married in 1958 after a short courtship. He was from New York City and moved to Montreal to be with me while I was finishing my teaching contract and getting my BA and teaching degree from Sir William University.

After my graduation, we bought a house near Somerville, New Jersey, where we settled and started our family. I never met David's parents; unfortunately, they had both died before we met.

I worked as a substitute teacher until I became pregnant, but once I started showing I was no longer permitted to teach. David had inherited a plumbing supply store in the Bronx, but he was not interested in the business, so he sold it after we moved to New Jersey.

While living in Hillsborough, we joined a temple in Somerville and met a group of other young couples that we socialized with. Both David and I were involved in the temple. David was the vice president, while I got the job of corresponding secretary. We enjoyed entertaining in our home. We had lavish dinner parties and a nice group of friends, most of whom had children, while we were just starting our family.

Our first child, a daughter, was born at Somerset Hospital. Michelle was a tiny baby with big brown eyes and a full head of black hair—the most beautiful baby that any parent could wish for. She was a quick learner and she loved books. We had to read to her all the time, over and over.

When Michelle was eighteen months old, another beautiful baby girl was born. Laura had blue eyes and light brown hair. She was a real charmer and she smiled all the time. Like Michelle, Laura was a quick learner. At times, Michelle resented having a baby sister; she did not want the competition. As they grew older, they enjoyed each others' company and liked playing together. From an early age, Laura loved to draw and showed a lot of talent in art.

I enjoyed dressing the girls alike in beautiful outfits. Often we were asked if they were twins. It was a joy to have two little girls to dress and watch them grow up.

Eighteen months after Laura's birth, along came a darling little boy. Glen, like his sisters, was born by Caesarean section at Somerset Hospital. While at the hospital prior to giving birth the physician informed me that she heard two heartbeats and I was having twins, but it was a false alarm—only one child was born, a blue-eyed baby boy with very little hair.

The girls were very happy to have a little brother and David and I were delighted to have a son. Glen was a good, healthy child and we all loved babying him, especially his two older sisters. In a sense they were a little jealous and claimed that we favored him. In reality, the girls doted on him; he was like a toy to them and they enjoyed playing with him. When he got a little older, they did not like him getting into their toys and other things. Glen grew to be a fast learner and he enjoyed school and various other activities.

It was a sheer delight to see them growing up together, even though at times it was hard work raising three children so close in age. The children were the joy of my life. They were all good students and it was a pleasure to get rave reviews from the teachers whenever David and I attended parent-teacher conferences. All three children continued to do very well in high school and college, and went on to earn advanced degrees and became responsible adults in their communities.

Once the children were in school, I decided to sign up to become a substitute teacher in Columbia, Maryland. It was a different experience from teaching my own class. We enjoyed living in Columbia, close to Washington, DC, and we made many trips there to museums, concerts and sightseeing.

Eventually, David was transferred to Arizona. At this point I had no desire to teach any more and thus enrolled in graduate school at Arizona State University (ASU). Initially, I was in the graduate school of foreign languages where I studied French Literature. Subsequently I transferred to the graduate program of social work where I received a master's degree in 1977. I worked for the Department of Economic Security in Phoenix, Arizona. I was doing investigations for Child Protective Services for 13 years and Adult Protective Services for 10 years. I enjoyed my work very much. It was challenging and stimulating to work with the courts and numerous professionals in the community.

I retired in 2000 and began to travel. I went to China with a group of mostly teachers and enjoyed the trip very much. I also went to Bangkok, Hong Kong, Australia and New Zealand. I began doing volunteer work, and became a peer counselor in Scottsdale, Arizona after my retirement.

At the time, I was already divorced from David and the children had left home to pursue their studies and careers. David and I remain on friendly terms and we have shared many happy occasions with our children. We attended graduations, weddings and celebrated the births of our grandchildren together.

Michelle, Laura and Glen are all happily married and each has two children. At the time I am writing this, Michelle and her husband Scott's daughter Isabel is 16, and their son Alex is 15. Laura and Ken's daughter Anna is 13 and Jack is 10, while Glen and his wife Lauren have Zachary, 11, and Lindsey, 9. I adore my children, their spouses and my grandchildren. I am very proud of their accomplishments and they are very good to me. I am lucky that they all live in California, which permits me to have more contact with them now than when I resided in Arizona five years ago.

I feel that I have come a long way since my existence in the small, primitive village of Okuniew in Poland. My life in Okuniew was simple but happy, surrounded by my family, my dear parents and siblings. Of course, all this drastically changed when Hitler invaded Poland on September 1, 1939. Our lives were shattered and destroyed forever. The loss of my family was devastating.

Nevertheless, I survived and I am a testimony to what happened during the years of Hitler's attempted genocide on the Jewish people. I picked myself up and decided to go on living. I made a new life for myself, a life that has given me much happiness and a promise for a future and hope in the United States of America. I have come to the conclusion that any person can overcome obstacles in life with determination, a strong will and a willingness to work hard.

I overcame the obstacle of learning a new language, got an education and began teaching school at the age of eighteen. I married a Jewish American man and had a good marriage and family, which was my pride and joy. I have three great children, with their spouses, and six wonderful grandchildren.

My life has included travel, and I have enjoyed friends and numerous cultural activities. I love the theatre, plays, dance and concerts. I enjoy the outdoors and was an avid hiker in my younger days in the Canadian Rockies, the Grand Tetons and the Grand Canyon. I still enjoy physical activities and go to the gym as often as time permits.

In spite of all this, I still miss my family, so much so that it took me fifty years before I could speak in public about my personal past and the Holocaust. We survivors are caught between the living and the dead. We continue to lament our families who perished.

The Holocaust is now history. It happened a long time ago, yet it is difficult to understand that this could have happened to human beings in the 20th century. It is incomprehensible: the mass murder of Jews and others on such a large scale. André Malraux summed it up well: "This was the century that killed men."

In 2003, I arrived in Santa Barbara, California, and became involved with the Jewish Federation of Greater Santa Barbara, where my story is featured in a permanent exhibit, *Portraits of Survival: Life Journeys during the Holocaust and Beyond*.

I am now a volunteer and docent for the *Portraits* exhibit and speak to many groups of all ages about my experiences, growing up in Poland and as a first-hand witness to the Holocaust. Groups of schoolchildren visit the exhibit and my fellow survivors and I talk to them about our lives and our personal histories. We also go to schools to tell our stories and give presentations.

It has become much easier for me to share my experiences now, and it has helped me to deal with the past. I have become aware of how important it is to inform young people about how destructive and damaging anti-Semitism can be, and prejudice of any kind. It is imperative that we teach the new generation to be kind and accepting of people of different religions and race. The world is in great turmoil; it is my hope that we can build a better world of peace for our children, our grandchildren and all mankind. That is why I am sharing my story.

Epilogue II

ᐤRevisiting the Past

IN 1996 I TRAVELED to Poland, Czechoslovakia, and Hungary with the Jewish Heritage Travel Group. My family did not want me to return there in the event that the Polish government would detain me, as I had left Poland illegally. Nevertheless, I wanted to return to Eastern Europe, to visit my home and see what was left after the devastation of the war years. I needed to find out if there were any memories for me still in Okuniew; it was unfinished business until I returned to see for myself. Of course, I was apprehensive and nostalgic at the same time about my return. After all, my loved ones are gone and everything I knew had been destroyed.

Our first stop was Warsaw. Warsaw has been rebuilt since the destruction of the city during World War II. It is even more beautiful than it was before I left, which was after the demolition of the Warsaw Ghetto. I went to the Jewish cemetery to see if I could find the graves of any family members who may have been buried there. To my great disappointment, I did not find anyone I knew. I also wanted to find the remains of the Warsaw Ghetto, and this was another disappointment: the ghetto was hidden beneath the courtyard of an apartment building. A monument had been erected in the plaza in memory of those who perished in the Ghetto.

Afterwards, I took a walk to Mickiewicz Park where there was a Chopin concert in progress. I visited the magnificent palace and took a ride in a horse-drawn coach. When I got hungry, I went into a small pub to have some lunch. I have always enjoyed some of the Polish specialities. The afternoon was almost idyllic, despite the devastation and bad memories all around me.

I asked the tour guide from our trip if I could hire her to take me to Okuniew for a visit. She agreed. We set out after breakfast in her small car. I was surprised to find out that the whole trip was a mere 10 miles. It had seemed so much longer when I was a child! I was nervous and had a lot of mixed feelings about going back to my village where no one in my family was alive. On the other hand, I was hopeful to find some familiar faces that could shed a little light on what they knew about the destruction of all the Jews in Okuniew.

Once again, I was disappointed. We did not find anyone or anything from my childhood that was left there. The synagogue was gone; my home as well as the homes of my uncles and grandfather were destroyed.

Our next venture was to find the Jewish cemetery where my grandfather was buried. This was heartbreaking for me; the Jewish cemetery was completely leveled and overgrown with weeds. On the other hand, the Catholic Church and cemetery were intact and beautifully groomed. I remember, as a little girl, how worshippers always gathered on Sunday outside the sanctuary following mass.

We walked around town trying to find some familiar faces. No one was alive that I knew before the war. In fact, Okuniew had not changed very much.

On to Czechoslovakia. We went to see the Terezin concentration camp, near Prague. Thousands of Jews died there, mainly children. The following day we drove to the Auschwitz concentration camp. What an irony: at the entrance of the camp there is a big sign "Arbeit macht frei", "Work makes you free." This was a very somber day indeed, walking through the camp where millions of Jews and others died in the most brutal way; it was heartbreaking. The cruelty human beings had to endure is unbelievable.

In our group were a few survivors. One daughter was on the trip with her father who had been in the camp; she sobbed uncontrollably when he pointed out to her where he was housed. A couple of Hungarian women pointed out to us the bunk beds they slept in at Birkenau, an absolutely horrible and depressing place. These same ladies pointed out the tall wire fences against which many women threw themselves to commit suicide by electrocution—when they no longer were able to cope with the cruel treatment committed by the German guards.

When we went through the exhibit where they housed hundreds of the victims' eye glasses, suitcases, shoes and hair, I had to step outside. In sadness I visualized the discarded items belonging to my family members.

At the end of my trip, I flew to Warsaw from Budapest to visit Wanda and her family. I was met at the airport by Wanda, her son-in-law Riszu and Wanda's teenage granddaughter Agnieszka. The reunion was very emotional. We had not seen each other since I departed Bydgoszcz in 1948.

Wanda and I sat in the back seat of the car holding hands and sitting very close to each other. Riszu drove us all the way to Torun where he and his family live. I met Wanda's beautiful daughter Mariola and we spent a few days in her home. I felt very comfortable with Wanda's family; they are kind, gentle people and very good to me. Wanda's son Jurek and his wife Basia joined us for dinner. It was a very happy time for reminiscing. No one spoke English; Agnieszka had a little knowledge of it, so I had to recapture my Polish in a hurry. It was amazing how, after a day or two, I started to remember more and more Polish words. After two weeks I was nearly fluent to an extent.

After our brief stay with Mariola, Riszu and Agnieszka , Wanda and I returned to Bydgoszcz. I could not believe that Wanda was still living in the same apartment on the third floor without an elevator. As we were walking up the stairs, Wanda pointed out some of the neighbors from when I lived with her that still live there. It was very nostalgic for me to be back in Bydgoszcz after so many years.

The following day I went downstairs to see what I still remembered from my past. Wanda was concerned that I might get lost, but I assured her that I am a big girl now. I had fun exploring the familiar sights. I went to the bakery and came back with some sweets and bread for our breakfast.

Bydgoszcz had not changed much since I left in 1948. When I went to the bank to change some American money for Polish zlotys,

I became aware of the lack of progress as compared to the United States. I saw this in the various shops as well, which were not modern and very old-fashioned.

Wanda took me to the old school where I first attended classes after 1945, and it looked a little run down. Later that evening we went to the church where I took my first communion. The mass in progress did not inspire much emotion in me; however, I went through the motions as best as I could. Wanda and I never discussed religion; she did not ask and I did not tell her anything about my return to Judaism. We were just happy to be together and enjoy the time we had.

We spent a few days in Torun with Wanda's daughter prior to my return to the United States. Torun is a historical town and we visited the Copernicus Museum, one of the earliest planetariums in the history of astronomy.

When it was time to leave, Wanda asked me if I could stay longer, but it was time to return to my job in Arizona. After my return home, Wanda and I stayed in touch. We correspond and at Christmas I send packages for the family. I have invited Wanda to visit me on several occasions, but she has never been able to visit me. Wanda saved all the letters I wrote to her for the past fifty years. We read them and I was amazed how well I could write in Polish. She was willing to part with the letters and gave them to me. At that point, I felt I never wanted to go back to Poland. The memories still haunted me, and I felt I had returned and seen what I needed to see.

Then, as it happened, in June 2007, Dr. Elizabeth Wolfson of the Jewish Federation of Greater Santa Barbara was invited to make a presentation at Jagiellonska University in Krakow, about the *Portraits of Survival* exhibit at the Jewish Community Center in Santa Barbara. Dr. Wolfson asked me to be her co-presenter at the conference because I am a participant in the exhibit and an exhibit docent. I thought this was another opportunity to revisit Wanda and her wonderful family. My friend Erika Kahn, another survivor and docent, also came to join the presentation. Our visit was a wonderful experience: we met students from all over the world who came to study and learn about the long-range effects of the Holocaust on the survivors, refugees and subsequent generations. The students were so receptive to our presentation and so eager to hear what we had to say that we scheduled extra time to meet with them over the weekend. In the end, we made many new friends and initiated new relationships; there were many hugs and we shared many photographs.

Following the conference, a group of students and professors went to Lublin for a few days I joined them. We went sightseeing, ate together and saw the remains of the Ghetto in Lublin.

We all went to see one of the largest concentration camps in Europe.

Majdanek: Another sad place. Near the entrance there is a large mound of human ashes. We were able to view the crematoriums where so many died.

From Lublin I decided to take the train to visit Wanda in Bydgoszcz. Wanda and her son Jurek and his wife Basia met me at the train station. They had a car and I also appreciated that they carried all the baggage.

Jurek drove us to Wanda's apartment on Jagelonska Street. Some of the pavement was torn up as they were doing urban renewal in the area.

Once again it was a happy reunion with Wanda. Basia and Jurek invited us for tea the following day. Wanda and I took the bus to their house in the morning. Basia bought all kinds of delicious pastries and she set a beautiful table in their luscious green garden.

I mentioned to Basia and Wanda that I would like to revisit my old school. Since Basia teaches part-time at the school and she knows the principal and the teachers, she made arrangement for us to go there. Jurek and Basia picked us up and we drove to the school. This was truly the hightlight of my trip. We had the most wonderful reception from the principal and teachers: they just could not do enough for me. They took me on a tour of the school and we visited my old classroom. They pulled out yearbooks and pictures from the time when I attended—in 1945 and after. I also got a beautiful souvenir of an illustrated book of the school.

Jurek waited for us outside the school, and when we finished he drove us to a quaint restaurant for lunch. We went back to Jurek's and Basia's home for a snack and later Jurek drove us to the church where Wanda and I used to worship.

I did not recognize the building; it was a magnificent new structure, much larger than before; it looked more like a cathedral. There was a mass in progress. Wanda, Basia and I walked in while Jurek waited outside for us. We stayed in the church for a little while and then joined Jurek who drove us back to Bydgoszcz.

Then Jurek offered to drive Wanda and me to Torun to visit with Mariola and her husband Riszu. They had built a beautiful home on the outskirts of Torun, surrounded by a forest. The home was elegantly furnished and had a large bright kitchen with modern conveniences.

I got the guest of honor bedroom: large and bright. Wanda and I enjoyed our daily walks in the adjoining woods. Mariola made delicious meals for us. Mariola and her husband took me to the flea market and supermarket as well. The supermarket was very large with lots of aisles stacked with all kinds of gourmet foods—quite a big change from my last visit, twelve years ago.

As they say, "all good things come to an end." Once again it was time to return home. Tomek, Agnieszka's boyfriend offered to drive us back to Bydgoszcz.

Wanda and I went into town one day and I bought an airline ticket to Warsaw. The following morning we had a taxi pick us up for the airport. Wanda wanted to see me off, so she went along with me to the airport.

I had no plans to return to Poland any time soon; however, as I write this, I am getting ready to leave for Poland once again, on August 6, 2008. Why the sudden change of heart? A few days ago I received a letter from the Israeli Embassy in Warsaw informing me that my rescuer Wanda Handrysiak and her husband Telesfor Handrysiak have been recognized as "Righteous among the Nations" by the Israeli Embassy in Warsaw and Yad Vashem, the Holocaust Museum in Israel. On August 10 they will receive an award in Bydgoszcz. I owe Wanda my life and I would not miss the opportunity to witness this wonderful presentation—for anything in the world. I would not be here to write my memoir if it was not for Wanda and her husband. They risked their lives to save me and I will forever be grateful to them.

Ceremony for Wanda in Bydgoszcz

WHEN I RECEIVED the invitation from the Israeli Embassy in Warsaw, I was in a real quandary whether to go to Poland or not. However, I started to think about what Wanda did for me to save my life and I came to the conclusion that I must go. Immediately I began to call various airlines to inquire about the cost of the fares. The fares were all costly but I purchased my tickets from Lufthansa Airlines. My flight would take me from Los Angeles to Frankfurt with a transfer to Warsaw. On August 6, 2008 I took the airbus shuttle from Santa Barbara to Los Angeles International Airport. The driver dropped me off at the Bradley International Terminal. I immediately got in line at the Lufthansa check-in for Frankfurt, Germany. I was amazed to see so many security people with machine guns displayed right next to the check-in. The line was long and crowded. Many passengers were in line with carts piled up high with suitcases. I finally checked in and had some spare time to check out the duty- free shops and get some lunch.

Now it was time to go through security where we take off our shoes and got rid of the water bottle. We stood in line until our turn came to be cleared. The lines were long and tiring, and I was glad when we were able to go to the waiting room to sit until boarding time was to be announced. After a while I got a little hungry, so I asked one of my fellow passengers to watch my belongings while I went to the snack bar to buy some food and drink. When I returned I got into a conversation with two ladies from California who were also traveling to Warsaw, Poland. We talked about our respective trips and it made the time go faster.

Finally we heard the loudspeaker announcement that it was time to board our plane to Frankfurt. I had never flown with Lufthansa Airlines and was very pleasantly surprised to find good service and fine young men and women in attendance. One large meal was served after we took off and settled down. We had a couple of snacks and the attendants came by with water quite often.

After eleven-and-a-half hours in the plane we landed in Frankfurt. It was time for me to get to the next terminal and find my connection to Warsaw. Prior to boarding the plane to Warsaw we had to go through security, I was worried that I might miss my connection. However, with a little assistance from a stewardess, I made it to my gate in time. The plane to Warsaw was operated by Polish Lot Airlines. I was seated next to a Polish businessman who spoke English very well, so we had some interesting conversations about America and Poland. After ninety minutes we arrived in Warsaw. We went through security again. After we got our baggage, it was very easy and I was on my way to find Wanda and her family.

There is always a big crowd waiting outside for relatives and friends. I was delighted when I spotted Mariola waiting for me; Mariola is Wanda's daughter. She gave me a big hug and whisked me outside to find her husband Riszu, with the car. Riszu greeted me affectionately and put the bags in the trunk of the car and we set out for Torun where Wanda was waiting for us.

We chatted all the way home even though I was very tired. Mariola called Wanda to let her know that we are on our way home. It took us a little over four hours to reach Torun. I was very excited to see Wanda again. She looked radiant and very happy that we were together again.

Agnieszka arrived home from work and she joined us for dinner. A lot of questions were asked at the dinner table and I felt a little tongue-tied trying to get my Polish words out.

The following evening we all went to town for dinner. Agnieszka works in Torun and she found a restaurant that specializes in pierogy which I adore. We all sat down in the restaurant and ordered dinner.

All of a sudden it started to rain and it got very dark and stormy. The family was frightened, so we asked the waitress to pack up our dinner to take home and we left in a big hurry to find the car. We returned home quickly before the thunder and lightning started.

On Saturday morning we set out for Bydgoszcz with Tamasz and Agnieszka. Wanda had called the beauty parlor and we got appointments to get our hair done for the big occasion. On Sunday morning around nine Wanda's family arrived at the apartment. Everyone looked beautiful: the ladies had on pretty outfits and the men looked very handsome in their suits and ties.

Wanda and I were a little nervous not knowing what to expect. The car trunk was full of bouquets of flowers for Wanda and me. When we arrived at the building where the ceremony was to take place, we were greeted by officials from the city of Bydgoszcz and the representative from the Israeli Embassy. Young women escorted us to our VIP seats next to the stage.

As soon as we arrived at our seats, we were invaded by reporters from numerous newspapers, television and radio. We were whisked away to be in front of television cameras prior to the commencement of the program. The program began with various speeches from the city officials and the introduction by the Israeli Embassy Wanda and I were asked to deliver our speeches to the audience. I was asked to go first. I decided to do my talk in Polish since it was a predominately Polish audience. Although my Polish is not very good I explained to the audience that I had forgotten to speak the language while living in the United States. The gist of my speech was about Wanda saving my life and I thanked her for doing so. I started off by saying that I am alive because Wanda saved my life. Interestingly enough, many of the newspapers quoted me using my exact words. Following me Wanda was asked to deliver her speech. She said some very nice things about me, and told how I came to Warsaw to live with her and her husband when I was seven years old.

The Israeli ambassador was the only person who spoke in English; his assistant translated. We shook hands with the ambassador and he handed Wanda the medal and diploma. The ambassador quoted that "He who saves one life saves the whole world". We also had two young musicians from the Music Academy in Bydgoszcz. They played beautiful music suitable for the occasion. When the ceremony was finished, we were invited for a reception downstairs for refreshments and conversation with the invited guests. Afterwards, Wanda's family decided that we all should go to a nearby café for dessert and coffee. It was very pleasant and everybody commented what a nice ceremony it was.

Wanda and I were then driven to her apartment to change and we drove with Jurek and Basia to their home for dinner. Basia is an excellent cook and she served a beautiful meal on the indoor porch. After dinner we watched the television program of the festivities. Then Jurek and Basia drove us back to Bydgoszcz. Wanda and I looked at all the things that we had received at the ceremony. We were quite tired and went to bed early. Next morning, while I was still sleeping, Wanda went downstairs to buy the various newspapers with articles about the ceremony and interviews with various people. Wanda received another call from a reporter asking for an interview with both of us. We invited the reporter to come to Wanda's apartment on the Tuesday morning before we left for our trip to Torun.

Yurek and Basia came to pick us up at the apartment and took us both to Wanda's daughter in Torun. We stayed there for a couple of days so we could take the train to Warsaw on August 13, prior to my departure for the United States on the 14th. Mariola made a nice dinner and Wanda and I went for a walk in the woods. After dinner I packed my luggage as Tomasz was coming to get it before Wanda and I took the train to Warsaw. Mariola and Ryszu took us to the train and found us a compartment to sit in; some other people joined us in the compartment until we arrived at the train station in Warsaw. Wanda called Agnieszka when we arrived and in a few minutes she came to pick us up while Tomasz waited in the car for us. Tomasz drove us to the hotel where I registered for the night and we left our luggage there.

We all went to town to visit the monument to the Warsaw Ghetto heroes. We walked up the steps of the monument and found a large number of votive candles called "Yartzeit candles", as well as various messages written on paper and small rocks. That inspired me to write a message myself to honor my family as well. I found a small rock in the area and went to the car to fetch a pen and write a few words in memory of my parents and siblings.

We took pictures at the monument and also walked around to the site where there is being built a museum for the Holocaust. Then Wanda and I wanted to see our old apartment which was near the ghetto area.

Tomash drove us to Muranowska St. number 14. Unfortunately the building where we lived had been destroyed in a fire. In its place a modern high rise was being built. The four of us went out to dinner, to a quaint restaurant that specializes in pierogy. The restaurant made each order separately and we could have a choice of many different fillings, they were delicious, much better than the ones we had in Torun.

Tomasz and Agnieszka took us back to the hotel for the night and also picked us up in the morning of August 14 to go to the airport.

Wanda and Agnieszka wanted to see me off while Tomasz stayed with the car. The lines were very short this time and in no time I was going through security. The trip to Frankfurt and Los Angeles was uneventful and I arrived at Los Angeles International Airport on time. I got my bags and went through a very brief security check.

I just missed my airbus to Santa Barbara, thus went to have a bite to eat, made some phone calls to the family to let them know I was back safe.

I arrived in Goleta and was picked up by my friend Judy. It is always good to be home; I opened some of my mail, took a shower and went to sleep. Of course, jet lag hit and I was up in the middle of the night, but that too soon passed.

A week later, I decided to visit my son Glen and his family in Palo Alto. I took the train and had a pleasant trip to San Jose. It was good to see my daughter-in-law Lauren and my two grandchildren Zachary and Lindsey.

The following day Lindsey and I walked over to the drug store and supermarket. On our way home we met two ladies walking a cute little dog. Lindsey bent over and started to pet the dog. I asked if it was OK for my granddaughter to pet the dog and they agreed that it was. When I asked the name of the dog, Naomi told me it was Pushkin, so

I wanted to know if Pushkin was Russian and Naomi told me no, that it was Polish, her husband is Polish, he was born in Warsaw in 1939.

I let Naomi know that I had just returned from Poland, she asked for my telephone number for her husband, Dr. Robert Mindelzun. I told Naomi that I was visiting my son and told her the street that he lived on. Coincidentally, she lived on the same street. Lindsey and I arrived home and shared our encounter with my son and daughter-in-law. They let me know that they knew who Naomi and Dr. Mindelzun were and that they had been to their house. My son suggested that on Sunday we go to visit Robert.

As time progressed Bob and I discovered that we followed the same path in Poland just before the war ended and after. Bob, like I, was liberated in Krakow in 1945. He then went with his family to Bydgoszcz where he attended school. I told Bob that last year I went to visit the school and took some pictures. Bob wanted to see the pictures however they were at my home in Santa Barbara. When I returned home I found the pictures and my grade certificate from the school. To make a long story short, we discovered that we went to the same school at the same time after the war. Bob is several years younger than I am. We continue to e-mail each other and will visit next time I return to Palo Alto. This entire wonderful encounter happened because we were taken by a cute little dog named Pushkin!

Made in the USA
Charleston, SC
16 February 2010